My MOTHER MARRIED MY Rapist

SHERRI MARIE

Acknowledgments

First, I would like to thank God for giving me the strength to write my life story. Thank you for turning my life experiences into my purpose and testimony. Secondly, I would like to thank all my readers and supporters. I want to thank all of you for believing in me and supporting all my work.

Finally, to all my children, Davonna, Quanterrious, Makayla, and Promise. I want to let y'all know that I love you with all my heart. Y'all are the reason I'm the woman I am today. I wouldn't trade you for anything in the world. Y'all made me stronger and taught me the true definition of love. I will go through hell and high water for each of you. When God made y'all, he knew exactly what he was doing, He made y'all just for me. I will always have y'all back no matter what. I love all of you to the death of me, and that's on my life. Love, Mommy (Davonna, stop crying lol.)

To my father, Daniel Neal, thank you for believing in me when nobody else did. Thank you for encouraging me to never give up on my dreams. At times I wanted to quit writing, and you told me to keep pushing. You always know the right words to say when I'm down and out. Whenever I need something, no matter what it is, you always have my back. If I can't count on anyone else, I know I can always count on you. You protected me and made sure you kept me away from any harm or danger. You are the world's greatest father, and I am happy to call you my dad. I love you, Daddy, always and forever in my heart.

Marcus, thank you for being such a loving man to my children and me. Thank you for loving me unconditionally and sticking by me when I was at my lowest. You always taught me how to love and keep the faith. Even when I lost my faith, you would give me encouraging words to regain it. God couldn't have sent me a better man. You are heaven-sent and a blessing to me. You're my best friend, my lover, my soulmate, my #1 supporter, my everything, and so much more. I could write a book about you, but you know what it is. I love you always and forever, baby.

Ravine Neal, my niecy pooh, my stinka butt, lol. I love you so much, and there is nothing in the world that I wouldn't do for you. I have watched you grow from a little girl to a beautiful, crazy young lady, lo. I just want to say that I love you with all my heart, and that will never change. Dymond and Daniel, my beautiful niece and handsome nephew, I know y'all have been through a lot these last couple of years. I just want to say I love you, and I'm here for you both if y'all ever need me. I love both of you from the bottom of my heart.

Lakeyshia Dennis (Kee), my cousin, my best friend, my right hand. You have been there for me since day one. You watched my struggles and witnessed almost everything I have been through. When I told you everything I went through as a little girl, you cried because you felt my pain. I just want to say thank you for your love and support. You always had my back no matter what, and I love you for that. You never judge me, and you always stuck by my side. When I'm down, you always lift me up with a prayer. That's why I call you my prayer warrior. Through ups and downs, right and wrong, you will always be my day one.

You watched me go through so many tragic things in my life, and you were there to keep me uplifted. When I cried, you cried. When I fought, you fought. When I hurt, you hurt. I wouldn't trade you for anything in the world. You helped me overcome a lot of my struggles, and I thank you for that. You will always be my day one, Love you cousin, always.

Terri Lucas (Twin)—Thank you for being my niece/best friend. We've been through so much together. When I needed someone to vent to or a shoulder to cry on, you were always there. We had a lot a of good and fun times together. I'm glad that God placed you in my life. Thank you for your love and support. I love you with all my heart. Don't forget that (wink).

Davida Mason, thank you for being such a great friend to me. Through ups and downs, you always had my back. We had so many good times together and more to come. Whenever I needed somebody to talk to, your ears were always open, and when I needed someone to be petty with, you were always down, lol. Thank God we grew up! Thank you for your love and support. I love you, bestie.

Aunt Carla, thank you for being a mother figure in my life. Whenever I need a shoulder to lean on or an ear to listen, you were always there. I just want to say thank you from the bottom of my heart, and I appreciate you.

Chaunette Singleton, my sister from another mister. I know we had our ups and downs, but you will always be my sissy. You and I both faced some tragic times in our lives when we were younger, and that brought us even closer. I just want to say I love you always and thank you for being a part of my life.

Jayvon Leonard, where do I start with you? My brother from another mother. You definitely made a big impact on my life, man. When I'm down, you always know the right words to say to make me laugh. You always got my back no matter what, and I love you for that. When I told you my plans for the future, you had my back 100% and gave me some good feedback. You are the true definition of a friend and brother. I love you always, no matter what, no one can come between that.

Esther Brooks, although you're not my biological grandma, blood couldn't make us any closer. After I began dating your grandson, Marcus, we became very close. You accepted my kids and me as if we were your own grandkids, and I appreciate you for that. Whenever I need to talk or vent, you are always there to listen. You are never judgmental, and you always keep it real with me, no matter what. I love you, Grandma, always and forever.

Rosalyn Smith, we had our ups and downs in the beginning. As time went on, we grew to love each other. Thank you for being such a wonderful mother-in-law to me. I love you with all my heart, and I wouldn't trade you for anything in the world.

Michael Smith, my loving, caring, sweet, brother in law. You are the little brother I always prayed for. I love you from the bottom of my heart.

Aundray Sanders, my brother. If anyone knows my struggle, it would be you. You watched me grow from a little girl into a young lady. Whenever I needed you, you were always there. If I called and told you some-body was messing with your little big sister, as you call me, lol, you came running to my rescue. You even stood in front of a gun for me. Through ups and downs, you always had my back, and I salute you for that. No one can ever take your place. Love, your little big sister.

Fred Brown, I love you always and forever. You always had my back no matter what the situation was. There would be times when I would cry, and you would tell me to wipe my tears asap, lol. When I needed advice, you kept it all the way real with me, whether I liked it or not. You are the true definition of a real friend, and I will always love you, no matter what.

Romel Sorrells, my brother from another mother, bka little man. Lol, just kidding. When we first met, we instantly clicked like brother and sister. When I found out you were a Pisces, you really became the homey. Every time we see each other, we're always capping and making short jokes. Marcus says we act like Martin and Pam, lol. I just want to say thank you for being a part of my life. I love you always.

Lakida "Crazy" Cannon, I met you when you started messing with Romel years ago. Over time, we became very close, and I don't regret it one bit. I can talk to you about any and everything. It feels like I've known you all my life, and it has only been a couple of years. I just want to say thank you for being a true friend. I love you always and forever.

Natasha Stewart and Saint Stewart, thank you for believing in me and sticking by my side. I love both of you with all my heart.

Danyell Love, my beautiful daughter-in-law. I love you so much, with your crazy self, lol.

To all my family and friends, I love all of you from the bottom of my heart. If I forgot anyone, I truly apologize.

Thinking Out Loud

Who would have thought I would be telling my story today? Not me. For years, I struggled to write my life story. I was so hurt and embarrassed by my life, and I thought that no one would care. I cried out for help, but no one heard my cry. Do you know how it feels to cry for help, but no one is listening? Do you know how it feels to be touched like a grown woman when you're only eight or nine years old? Do you know how it feels for your mother to believe her man over you?

No child should ever have to experience sexual abuse. This is my story, and I have the right to speak my truth. For years, I protected my mother's feelings, even though she didn't protect mine. I hope my story will help or prevent someone from going through the tragedies I faced as a child.

I remember walking into a room at my mother's friend's house and seeing her and Patrick in the bed naked. I quickly shut the door and ran into the living room. Minutes later, my mother called my name. I went into the room to see what she wanted, and that's when Patrick began to whoop my ass like I stole something. When he was done beating me, he told me to knock next time. I didn't know this man from a can of paint, and I hated my mother for letting him put his hands on me like I was his child. My mother just stood there watching him beat me with a belt.

Patrick was a tall, dark-skinned guy, and he wasn't attractive at all. He stood about 6'2" with dark skin that looked like it had been burning in hell all his life. He weighed at least 230 to 250 pounds at the time. His nose was so wide that a train could travel through his nostrils. Everything about him screamed ugly. I didn't see what my mother saw in him because she was beautiful but to each his own.

We lived in Starkville, Mississippi, for a while. It took several months to adjust, but eventually, I did. My mother and Patrick got a townhouse together months later. It was hard for me to get used to another man being around because I was so used to my father.

After we had been in Mississippi for a while, my grandmother on my mom's side passed away. She was like another mother to me, and I loved her to death. My grandmother didn't take shit from anyone, and she damn sure didn't bite her tongue. She told the truth, whether you liked it or not. I guess it was the Pisces in her.

My mother was livid when she learned my grandmother didn't leave her a dime. From my understanding, my grandmother didn't approve of Patrick dating my mother. That's why she didn't leave her anything. From what I heard, Patrick was disrespectful to my granny and called her out of her name a couple times. My uncle Kenny didn't appreciate how Patrick was speaking to my grandma, so he stepped in. Patrick and my uncle had a bad argument, and things got really heated.

My grandmother couldn't stand Patrick, but who could blame her? Any man who could disrespect an elderly woman needed to be handled accordingly, even if it meant beating the dog shit out of him. When Patrick disrespected my grandmother, you would think my mother would take up for her, but instead, she was on Patrick's side. My grandmother tried to warn her and tell her what type of guy Patrick was, but my mother didn't want to hear it. Bonnie loved Patrick, and she refused to let anyone come between that.

After my grandmother's funeral, Patrick told my mother not to worry about anything because he was moving us to Atlanta, GA. We had to move away from our family because they were mad that my grandma

"Stop crying like a baby and go to your room."

Those were the words he said to me right after he tried to make me suck his penis.

Chapter Two
CRYING FOR HELP

I constantly told my mother what Patrick was doing to me, but it always fell on deaf ears. She didn't believe me when I told her the things that Patrick was doing. I didn't understand why she was choosing his side over mine, especially since I was only a child, and all I wanted was to be protected. I soaked my pillow every night with tears. Every day, I would ask God, why me? I felt like I didn't have anyone to protect me from the pain I was going through. Some nights, I was afraid to fall asleep because I didn't know what time Patrick was going to come into my room. I didn't have anyone to talk to or to tell about the situation that was going on.

I can't even tell you how many times I told my mother. I felt like no one would believe my truth, especially if my mother didn't. As a mother, she should've believed me instead of her man. I felt defenseless, lonely, and afraid. I wanted to tell my father, but my mother kept me away from him for a long time. At one point, she wouldn't let me call him, but she eventually relented. I was miserable, depressed, and I didn't understand why this was happening to me.

When I was ten years old, we ended up moving again to an apartment complex called Jamerson Place. I attended Indian Creek elementary school. That's when I met my best friend, Tashay, and we became thick as thieves. For a while, I didn't tell her what was going on with me. I was embarrassed and afraid to lose her as a friend. We were both young, and I didn't know how this would affect her. Plus, I didn't want her mother to stop her from coming around me or coming to my house.

A few months into my friendship with Tashay, I felt comfortable enough to confide in her about everything that Patrick was doing to me. Tashay was angry, crying, and she wanted to kill that motherfucker as much as I did. The sad part is, she showed more emotion and concern than my own mother. I expected my mother to cry before she did. My mother didn't show any type of emotion when I told her. She told me I was a liar and to stop lying on Patrick. One day, my mother said, *what Patrick want with you when he got me?* I told Tashay to promise me that she wouldn't tell anyone, and she promised that she wouldn't.

About a year and a half later, we moved from Jamerson Place Apartments because our apartment caught on fire. A teenage boy who lived a couple of doors down from us was playing with a match and accidentally set his mattress on fire. I was outside playing at the time. My mother was at work, and I didn't know where Patrick was. His car was parked outside, so I assumed he was in the house. Although I had time to run in and tell him to get out, I didn't. Instead, I prayed and hoped that he was in the house sleeping. A smile stretched across my face from ear to ear as I watched the fire spread rapidly through the units. I wasn't smiling because it was on fire; I was smiling because Patrick was finally about to burn in hell with his father, Satan.

The fire department rushed into all the townhouses to help people get out. When they rushed into our apartment, I was pissed off because I didn't want them to save Patrick. I wanted him to fry. The firefighter came back out of our apartment and told the other firefighters that the unit was clear. Can you imagine how livid I was when I learned that Patrick wasn't in there? I know it sounds harsh, but it can't be any worse than what I was experiencing. It already felt like I was living in hell, mentally and physically.

The Red Cross put us in a hotel for a while until my mother and Patrick found somewhere for us to live. We moved off Cleveland Ave, which is considered Zone 3 or The Swats. Tashay and I stayed in touch. On some weekends, we would spend a night at each other's house when our parents would allow us.

Chapter Three

The next year passed without any real changes in my life. Patrick was still molesting me, and my mother was still in denial. He went from touching my breasts to sucking on them. That was the most disgusting feeling in the world. Patrick's dark skin, big nose, and ugly face made me sick to my stomach. I remember crying while looking down at him and begging him to stop. He would keep going, and it disgusted me. I hated him so much that his voice made my skin crawl. I wanted him to die for what he was doing to me.

At only eleven years old, I didn't deserve to be touched like a grown woman. All I wanted was to live my life as a normal child. Patrick took that away from me, and I can never get that back. No matter how many times I told my mother, she wouldn't listen, and I was tired of it.

One day, I decided to take matters into my own hands. I told Tashay that I wanted Patrick dead, and she was more than happy to help me plan his death. I was tired of him coming into my room every night, so something had to be done. I knew it was only a matter of time before things got worse.

We talked to a couple of dudes who were deep in the streets and asked how much they would charge us to kill Patrick's trifling ass. At first, they looked at us like we lost our mind, but when I told them what Patrick was doing to me, they were ready to take action. All we had to do was come up with the money they were asking for. Tashay and I were broke as hell, and we didn't have a damn dime to our name. Sometimes we would get an allowance, but it wasn't enough to pay them off. I thought about stealing my mother's money, but it was in the bank, so I had to scratch that plan off my list.

I was hurt because all I wanted was to see Patrick die and burn in hell. Was that too much to ask? One day, Tashay decided to spend a night at my house. We had a ball dressing up, taking pictures, and talking about girl stuff. As the night went on, we went into my bedroom and listened to music. Tashay lay at the top of my bed while I lay at the bottom.

"Tashay, I wish I could live with you," I told her.

"I wish you could too."

Before we could even get the rest of our conversation out, my doorknob began to jiggle. I already knew it was Patrick trying to get into my room.

"Play sleep," I whispered to Tashay. I could see the fear in my friend's eyes.

Patrick kept trying to get in, but he couldn't. Seconds had gone by, and finally, the doorknob stopped shaking. Minutes later, the doorknob began to jiggle again. My heart was pounding fast, and I was scared shitless. No matter how many times Patrick came into my room, I was always terrified. I didn't know what he was going to do to me next. We both glanced at the door as Patrick tried to use a credit card to get in. We watched as the card slid in and out. When he realized that wasn't working, he went to get a butter knife.

Minutes later, my door came open, and we played sleep. I could feel him standing over me as I lay there, trying to keep still. I heard him walk over to Tashay, and I peeked to see what he was doing. Patrick pulled the cover from over Tashay and admired her immature body as she lay there in only her training bra and shorts. When he was done lusting over her, he pulled the cover off me and stared at me. I started moving like I was waking up, and he ran out of the room.

"I told you he be coming in my room and molesting me," I said to Tashay.

I could tell that she was shaken by what had

happened. That was the last time Tashay spent the night at my house.

Chapter Four
THE WORST DAY OF MY LIFE

My mother decided to marry my molester, and I hated her for it. Although I told her that I didn't want to be in the wedding, of course, she forced me. I hated him, and I hated her for what she was letting him do to me. I heard that love is blind, but damn, at some point, you must open your eyes. This man was nothing but a manipulator; even Stevie Wonder could see past his bullshit.

I remember getting dressed for my mother's wedding and putting on that ugly ass royal blue bridesmaid dress. The last thing I wanted to do was be part of anything that had to do with them. After telling my mother thousands of times that her man was touching me, she still hadn't bothered to do anything about it. Patrick used to tell my mother that I was just saying that because he didn't give me what I wanted, and that was a good enough answer for her.

Not one time did I smile as I walked down the aisle. Hell, I had nothing to smile about. I had tears built up, and it took everything in me not to let them fall. To see my mother give herself to this man, knowing what he did to me made me sick as hell. The part that disgusted me the most was when the pastor announced that Patrick could kiss the bride. Watching him tongue her down made me want to vomit, especially since he was sucking my breasts and rubbing my vagina only nights before.

I hated this man, and every night, I prayed that he would die in his sleep or have a bad car accident. I know I've used the word *hate* a lot, but that's how I felt at the time.

At the reception, I kept my distance from everyone. I didn't want to be bothered at all. It seemed that everyone around me was against me. After the wedding, I called Tashay, crying like a baby, because I knew my mother would never leave this man. The part that hurt me the most is my mother acted like she didn't care. She had to know the truth because I wasn't the first person to accuse him of being a molester.

My mother had learned that Patrick molested his first cousin. There were also rumors that he molested a couple of females in Starkville, Mississippi. Not only that, but I heard his sister's first child is his son. She even named her son after Patrick. How much of a coincidence is that? Out of all three of her brothers, why would she name him Patrick? You would've thought she would name him after the older brothers, not the youngest one. I'm not saying that Patrick is the father of his nephew, but it's a 75% chance that he is. Patrick and his nephew look so much alike that the shit is scary. Let his family tell it, it's just a rumor somebody started.

I didn't get it. Every time Patrick was accused of molestation, there was always an excuse, especially from my mother. It was like he had everyone hypnotized, except for me. I saw right through his fat, black ass. For years, I isolated myself in my room. I felt like a prisoner in my own mother's house. Some days I didn't eat because I didn't want to see their faces. When they were asleep was when I would sneak to the kitchen to eat.

Chapter Five

We moved again, a couple streets down from Cleveland Ave into some apartments. I was around eleven at the time. I started school at Crawford W Long. My first day, I was nervous as heck because I didn't know one person. Although I didn't know anyone, I was happy to be at school. I felt safe, and free from the molester. I hated staying in the house with Bonnie and Patrick; it drove me crazy. Looking at him made my skin crawl.

Some days, I would be so tired in class that I would fall asleep, but that was the only peaceful sleep I had. I didn't rest much at home because I was too busy watching my door like a prison guard. Every noise I heard made my heart drop because I just knew that it was Patrick coming into my bedroom.

My teacher asked me one day why I was sleeping so

much. I remember looking at her, and while fighting back tears, I told her that I didn't know. Part of me wanted to tell her, but the other part of me was convinced she wouldn't believe me. Plus, my mother always told me that what goes on in our house stays in our house. At school, I couldn't even focus on my class-work because of what was going on in my household. It affected me tremendously.

After school, I never went straight home, especially if I saw Patrick's car. When I did decide to go into the house, I would go straight to the shower. Afterward, I would go into my bedroom and lock my door. Although having my door locked didn't keep me safe, it did warn me when Patrick was coming. I would hear him tampering with my doorknob and prepare myself for the worst.

Patrick began to get frustrated with my doors being locked every night. He would tell my mother to make me keep my door open because he thought I was being sneaky. I even got my ass whooped by him for locking my door. My mother wouldn't defend me. Instead, she would tell me to stop locking my door because I didn't pay any bills around there. I still locked my door when I felt like it. I had to protect myself because she sure as hell wouldn't.

Patrick got upset when he realized I was still locking my door, so he removed the locking mechanism. No matter where we moved, he always found a way to get into my room or unlock my door. I used to think my mother feared Patrick because she never did anything to defend me. She let him beat me senseless half the time. It was bad enough that he came into my room every night and did whatever he wanted to me. The messed up part is that Bonnie pretended to be blind to it all.

Anyway, I ended up meeting a girl named Amber Ray, who went to Crawford Long. She was short, heavy-set, and she had the prettiest chubby face. Amber was super cool and fun to be around. We instantly clicked when we met. Amber and I would hook up after school sometimes to chill. She was always laughing, cracking jokes, and her smile could brighten up a room. She always carried a smile on her face, no matter what; Amber was the definition of positive energy.

As months went by, Amber began to miss days from school, and that wasn't like her. The days she did show up, I could tell she wasn't herself. Amber was now quiet, sad, or looking like she wanted to cry. I asked Amber a couple of times what was wrong, but she would never tell me. She would always say nothing or make up some type of excuse. I knew deep in my heart that something was wrong, but I couldn't put my finger on it.

One day, our teacher announced that Amber had died. According to rumors, Amber had gone to Six Flags with her family the night before and gotten on the rides, knowing she was pregnant. From my understanding, she was six to eight months, and the baby belonged to her stepfather. I had no idea that Amber was pregnant. My heart was broken when my classmates told me that. I didn't get to attend the funeral, but I heard it was very nice. Amber and her unborn child were in the casket together. I wish I could've seen her one last time, just to tell her how much I loved her. Even though we only knew each other for a year, it felt like forever.

The only memory I have of Amber is her beautiful smile, goofy laugh, and positive energy. Amber's passing left a big hole in my heart, and I still think of her to this day.

As time went on, I became friends with Shakira, Chandra, Keonna, and Tee. Shakira, Chandra, Keonna, and I were in the same class at Crawford Long. Tee was a couple years older than us, so she was in high school.

Shakira and I became very close, and I often stayed at her house on the weekends. When I felt the time was right, I told Shakira that my mother's man was molesting me. Shakira was devastated when I told her, and she began to scream. Ms. Jones, Shakira's mother, heard her scream and rushed into the room to check on us.

"What's going on? Why are y'all crying?" Ms. Jones asked.

Shakira told her mother everything that I told her. When she was done, her mother was as hurt as we were.

"Oh, my God! Did you tell your mother?" Shakira's mother asked with a look of concern on her face.

"Yes, but she didn't believe me."

She shook her head. "How long has this been going on?"

"Since I was eight years old."

"This has been going on entirely too long. I'm calling the police."

"No! I'm going to get a whooping. Please don't call. Plus, I don't want to go to foster care."

"Baby, you can't keep letting this happen to you. You're just a baby."

I cried until I convinced Ms. Jones not to call the police.

"If I can't call the police, I'm calling your mother."

Ms. Jones picked up her cordless phone and asked for my mother's number. She paced the floor as she waited for Bonnie to answer. Ms. Jones couldn't wait to give my mother a piece of her mind, and I couldn't either. Surprisingly, my mother didn't answer the phone.

"You're not going back home. You can live with me," Ms. Jones told me.

"My mother and her husband aren't going to let me."

Ms. Jones shook her head. The whole weekend, she tried to call my mother, but there was no answer. On Sunday afternoon, Ms. Jones took me home. She didn't want to, but she had no choice. I had to get ready for school the next day.

When we arrived at where I lived, Patrick was standing outside. I just knew Ms. Jones was about to whoop his ass. Patrick spoke to Ms. Jones, but she didn't respond. Instead, she rolled her eyes and gave Patrick the evilest look. If looks could kill, Patrick would've been dead. At the time, I wished looks could kill.

Shakira gave me a big hug, and I could tell she didn't want to let me go.

"Don't hesitate to call me if you need me," Ms. Jones said right before she gave me a hug.

"Okay," I said as I held back my tears.

I got out of the car then made my way into the house. After I put my bags in my room, I went to my mother's room. Bonnie was on the phone, running her mouth with somebody from the church. I spoke to her, then headed back to my room. I remember lying in bed, staring at the ceiling and wishing I was dead or away from everything. I felt hopeless and empty inside. I couldn't take it anymore.

The next day, I got the strength to ask my mother if I could live with Ms. Jones. Of course, she said no. My mother was pissed off at me for asking her that question, but I didn't care. I wanted to get away from her molesting husband as quickly as I could. I prayed that my mother would say yes because I was tired of being

Patrick went on to call us lying asses and stupid. We got into a heated argument, and Patrick pulled the van over on the side of the highway. He unbuckled his seatbelt and began to punch me in my face like I was a man. I was trying to fight back, but he was hitting me repeatedly in the face. I picked up a crowbar that was lying on the floor by my seat and swung it with everything in me, hitting Patrick in the head.

"Don't hit my man with that crowbar!" my mother yelled as she tried to take the crowbar from me.

"You want to keep talking back, get the fuck out, and walk home."

Patrick slid the van doors and pulled me out of the van. He threw me on the side of the highway and left me there like I was a piece of trash. I couldn't have been no older than twelve years old. You think my mother made him come back and get me? Hell no. She left me there, stranded like I was a piece of shit. For those who don't know, Atlanta has one of the busiest highways. I was terrified as hell. My eyes were swollen from Patrick hitting me, and I could barely see.

I remember a car pulling up on the side of me. It was a gray Cutlass. The dude asked me was I okay and did I need a ride. I told him yes because my mother's boyfriend beat me up and put me out on the highway. He said he couldn't help me and sped off. I felt helpless, with no one to call or run to. I walked to the nearest exit, which was miles away, so I could call my mother's friend collect. Thank God, she came to get me. My mother's friend let me stay at her house for a day or two before she told my mother to come and get me.

My eyes were swollen and turning black, not to mention I had a big blood clot in my right eye. My mother made me stay home from school until my eye got better. She didn't want the school to see me like that because Bonnie knew they would report it.

I hated being in my mother and Patrick's presence. The sound of his voice made me want to shoot him in the head; if I had a gun, I would have. What irked me the most was that he knew what he was doing to me, but he played the innocent role. It made me mad as hell when we went to church on Sundays, and he would worship God like he wasn't molesting me from Monday through Saturday. My mother was no better; she would be shouting all around the church like she's so holy. They were both the devil in disguise if you ask me.

When I did return to school, I decided to go to the counselor's office and report what was going on in my home. I was nervous because my mother had always told me not to discuss anything that happened at home, but I decided to talk to my school counselor, anyway. After I was done talking to the counselor, she called the police, and they swarmed into her office. My heart was racing because I didn't know what was about to happen.

"What's going on?" one of the officers asked.

"This young lady reported that she is being molested by her stepfather in her home," the counselor replied.

"Is this true?"

I nodded.

"You don't seem too sure about this. Did he do this to you or not? This is a serious accusation."

When he said that, I automatically felt like he didn't believe me. "Yeah, I think he did," I said, feeling confused. I was scared shitless and didn't know what to say.

"You think? Or you know? I need to know did he do this to you."

"Yes."

The officer talked to me for a while then told the counselor he was going to question Patrick. When he said that, I knew it was over for me. Patrick wasn't dumb by far. He was a good liar, manipulator, and he knew the law very well. I guess the police bought his story because they didn't arrest him.

I went home and got the ass whooping of my life.

WEEKS LATER, WE MOVED OVER ON BRAEBURN CIRCLE, next door to Patrick's mom. I guess they were trying to make sure I didn't tell anyone else what happened. That wasn't going to stop me.

Soon as Patrick touched me again, I reported it, and

he was arrested that same day. That was the best day of my life. I could finally get some rest without him sneaking into my room. My mother was upset that I had Patrick locked up, and she was walking around with an attitude.

Bonnie wouldn't speak to me for days. When she did talk to me, it was to blame me for Patrick being locked up. My mother was hurt that Patrick was in jail, but that didn't stop her from cheating on him. Bonnie started messing around with a dude named Ricky, who lived in the apartments that we had recently moved from. He was a nice guy and always looked after the kids in the neighborhood. I used to call him Uncle Ricky.

Ricky was tall, dark, and wore braids. He stood about 5'11" to 6ft with a mouth full of golds. He had to be about forty-three years old at the time. I used to see him speak and flirt with my mother sometimes. Bonnie would giggle at Ricky's flirtatious ways and go about her business. Never in a million years did I think she would cheat with the man because she was so stuck up under Patrick's ass. I was happy, to be honest, and I prayed that they would be together. I liked Ricky; he had a good heart and spirit. Some nights, I would wake up and look out the window, just to see if Mr. Ricky's car was parked outside. Some nights it would be and some nights it wouldn't.

Patrick was no better. He cheated on my mother numerous times, and I witnessed it. I even recall him grinding on one of his sister and cousin's friends when we stayed in Kirkwood.

One day, Bonnie went to visit Patrick in jail, and he had gotten beat up really bad.

"All because of you, they beat Patrick up and broke his neck. They don't like molesters in jail. This is all your fault. Now he has to wear a neck brace because of you," Bonnie nastily said as soon as she walked into the house.

She made me feel so horrible that I began to cry. Bonnie made me feel guilty for having Patrick locked up. I thought I did the right thing by having him put behind bars. When was Bonnie going to care about my feelings? When was Bonnie going to care about what was happening to me? Bonnie didn't care about what was best for me; she was only worried about what was best for her. If she wasn't happy, nobody was.

Patrick got out of jail, and I was furious, especially when my mother told me that we were moving again. I don't know how Patrick got out, but he did. I thought my mother was going to leave his perverted, ugly ass for Ricky, but she didn't. I guess my mother called it quits with Ricky because after the monster got out, I never heard anything else about him. Soon as Patrick got out, my mother told me that we were moving.

Days later, my mother told me I could visit my father in Ohio. I was happy as hell that I was getting a break from them, although it was only for a couple of weeks because it was break. I didn't care if it was for twenty-four hours, as long as I was away from those devils. I knew my mother only wanted me to leave, so the heat would get off Patrick's ass. Bonnie knew if I was in Cincinnati, the police and Children's Services couldn't question me.

After I visited my father, my mother let me visit him a couple more times after that for the holidays. I wanted to tell my father what Patrick was doing to me, but I knew my mother would stop me from seeing him. I remember one year my father came to pick me up with his new girlfriend and his stepson in the car. I had met Ms. Ava a couple of times and talked to her on the phone. Ms. Ava was kind, sweet, and she wasn't to be messed with. The crazy part is she and my mother had the same birthday, April 2nd, but they acted nothing alike.

Ms. Ava will beat your ass and anybody else's ass over her kids. She had four sons, Tony, Gevonate, Ron, and Deon. They were all cool and treated me like their little sister. I remember Deon crying all the way from Atlanta to Cincinnati because he couldn't get a hot wheel that he wanted from the gas station. I wanted to choke his little ass up and throw him out of the car while it was moving. I can laugh at it now, but back then, the shit wasn't funny.

I became very close to Ms. Ava to the point that I called her Ma. To be honest, she acted more like a mother than my mama did. Ms. Ava didn't take no shit, and she was crazy about all her kids, including me. Ma was crazy period, LOL, and that's what I loved about her. I knew nobody was going to mess with me or cause me any harm if Ma was around.

Over time, Deon and I became very close, especially when he grew out of his cry baby mode. Deon was spoiled as shit, and we couldn't blame nobody but Ma for it. He was the youngest son of four boys, and Ma gave him whatever he wanted. Deon and I both were born in 1984, but I was the oldest by a couple of months. My birthday is Feb 28th, and his is September 14th. Our bond became super tight, and nobody could break that.

My father dropped me back off after spring break. After that, I didn't see him for a while because my mother only let me go when she wanted to.

WEEKS BEFORE I WENT TO CINCINNATI, PATRICK AND I GOT into another heated argument. He would pick with me over the littlest stuff. I swear I think it used to turn his ugly ass on. I remember him coming into my room and cussing me out because I was on the phone late on the weekend. He began to punch on me like I was his enemy. I picked up an iron and a glass cup then busted him in the head with both. I was tired of him hitting and molesting me. It was time to fight back.

My mother didn't bother to break it up. Instead, she was screaming and telling me not to hit Patrick. She didn't bother to help me or protect me. The only thing she cared about was her man and his safety. Meanwhile, I was crying and fighting for my life. I was losing my mind in that damn house. I thought about killing myself so many times. All I wanted was to be loved and heard by my mother. Instead, she treated me like I wasn't shit. Whether she knew it or not, that shit hurt like hell.

I was tired of having my vagina fingered every night. I was tired of my breasts being sucked on. I was tired of him whispering in my ear and telling me to play with my clitoris and that it will make me feel good, and I was tired of him asking me if I ever had sex before. I was tired of getting my immature vagina ripped open by his fat ass fingers. I had been touched like a grown woman for years, and I was tired of it. I wanted to just take a bottle full of pills and die. So many times, I thought about killing myself, but something was holding me back. I even asked God to take my life.

At one point, I began to blame God for what was happening to me. I didn't understand why God was allowing this to happen. Out of all the little girls in the world, why did God choose me to experience this pain and trauma? I know that sounds harsh, but that's how I felt at the time. I was stressed, depressed, and miserable. My self-esteem was low, and I didn't feel pretty at all, although I was. I felt like a prisoner in my own home. I wouldn't come out of my room for nothing in the world. I hated looking at Patrick's trifling ass.

As time went on, Patrick started taking things to another level. After he would finger me, he would smell his fingers and suck my juices off. Most of the time, I would play sleep, but he knew I was faking it. He would whisper in my ear; *I know you're not sleep.*

I remember one night, Patrick was sneaking in my room, and my mother came out of her bedroom. Patrick ran so fast. I knew she saw him, but she was so blinded by his bullshit that she didn't acknowledge it. I was so tired of being touched, but I had no more fight in me and no one to fight for me. No matter how much I told Patrick no or to stop, he still did it. I used to try to fight him off, but that didn't faze him at all. So, what was a little girl like me supposed to do?

No one believed me, and all my family was in a different city. All I wanted to hear from my mother was, *I believe you.* Instead, I heard, *you're lying, what he wants with you, or I don't believe you.* I was sick of it. If I had a gun, I probably would have killed them both in their sleep.

Chapter Six
THIRTEEN YEARS OLD

Summer of 1997

My mother finally decided to let me go to Ohio again to visit my father for the summer. When I got off the Greyhound, my father was waiting with open arms. I ran straight into his arms and gave him a big hug. My father was so happy to see me that he didn't want to let me go. I felt safe and protected in my father's arms.

After we left the Greyhound station, my father took me to my sister's house since that was where I was staying for the summer. I wanted to stay with my father, but he worked a lot. My sister worked a lot also, but not as much as my father and brother, Don. I was happy to be in Cincinnati with my family and siblings. Truth is, I didn't want to go back to Atlanta. When I was in Cincinnati, I felt loved, and most importantly, I felt safe. Anyway, my sister had two nieces, who were twins named Tia and Mia. They were her best friend Deb's children. Although they weren't her real nieces, blood couldn't make them any closer.

Tia and I became very close while I was in the city. My sister lived in English Woods apartments, which is considered the projects. Tia and Mia lived out there also with their mom. When my sister was at work, sometimes Tia and I would take walks and have long talks. Some days, I would go to her house to chill, listen to music, and play Tetris. I was finally experiencing how it felt to be a preteen, and it felt damn good. I didn't have to worry about anyone taking that away from me. It felt good to know that I didn't have to watch my back, my bedroom door, or walk around in fear anymore.

The summer was going well until Tia told me that she and Mia were going to Virginia for the rest of the summer. I was salty because we had become very close over the short time I was there. I was closer to Tia than I was Mia, but I loved them both. Tia was the chill, sweet one, while Mia was the mean, evil, tomboyish twin. After they left, I stayed in the house watching movies, listening to music, and thinking.

One day, my sister was running late for work. As she was getting dressed, she told me that she was doing a double shift from 7:00 pm to 7:00 am, and she would call to check on me through the night. My sister's car was broken down at the time, so she was waiting for her ride to pick her up. Minutes later, there was a knock on the door. My sister told me she would see me in the morning then rushed out. I didn't see who she left with, but I assumed it was the person she was waiting for.

I lay on the couch and fell straight to sleep. I was sleeping good until a knock on the door disturbed my peace. It couldn't have been anyone for me, so I ignored it. I thought the person would go away, but they kept knocking.

"Who is it?" I yelled, aggravated because I was woken out of my sleep.

"Mike."

Hearing a male voice immediately put my guard up. I didn't trust anyone after what Patrick had been doing to me. I cracked the door open a little.

"Is Chelly here? I'm here to take her to work."

"She already left for work."

"You sure?"

"Yes, I'm sure."

"What's your name, and where you from?"

"I'm Sherri, Chelly's sister. I'm from Atlanta."

"Can I use the bathroom?" he asked.

At first, I hesitated because I didn't know him. He could've been a kidnapper, a molester, or a rapist for all I knew. But I assumed since he knew my sister, it was cool to let him in.

"Go ahead," I said and opened the door wider so he could come in.

When he was done using the bathroom, instead of leaving, he joined me on the couch. Mike asked my age, and I told him I was thirteen years old and would be fourteen on Feb 28th. Mike put his arms around me and started kissing my neck.

"You so sexy," he told me.

"Aren't you too old for me?" I responded and pushed him away.

"I'm only seventeen."

"Not interested."

I wasn't attracted to him or any other man. To be honest, I hated men. I felt like every man wanted to take advantage of me like Patrick did.

"Come on. You are so beautiful."

Those words made me feel good, I can't lie. My self-esteem was already low because of the sexual abuse I was going through. To hear a man tell me I was beautiful made me feel bubbly on the inside.

Somehow, Mike ended up spending the rest of the evening with me chilling and watching TV. He kept trying to convince me to have sex with him. I kept telling him I didn't want to, but he was persistent like Patrick. He wouldn't take no for an answer. I finally gave in because I was tired of him asking me, and I was tired of trying to push him off me.

Mike took me upstairs to the extra bedroom. He told

me to get on the floor since there wasn't a bed in the room. He told me that it wouldn't hurt, and he promised to take it slow. However, Mike didn't take my precious gift into consideration. He rammed his penis into me from the back and took advantage of my vagina. He never even asked me if it was my first time. I was crying and telling him to stop, but he kept going.

After Mike was done, he went into the bathroom to wipe himself off. I stared at the blood that was all over the floor, confused about where it came from. At first, I thought I came on my period, but I had just gone off a few weeks ago. I ran to the bathroom and quickly washed up. When I was done, Mike asked me to walk him to the door, and then he left.

Yes, Mike broke my virginity. Did I like it? Hell no. Did I enjoy it? Hell no. He seduced me into having sex with him, and I fell for it. I remember crying like a baby after he left. I felt stupid as hell for letting him take my virginity. It felt like my life was getting worse every time I turned around. For the rest of the night, I watched movies and called my friends in Atlanta. My vagina was so sore I could barely walk.

The next day, when my sister came home, she asked me if I wanted to ride with her somewhere. I told her, yeah. My sister said okay and went to take a nap. When she woke up, she made us something to eat, took a shower, then got dressed. Chelly had borrowed one of her friend's car for the day, so we wouldn't be stuck in the house. When my sister was done getting herself together, we left.

We pulled up in Moosewood Apartments minutes later and made our way to her friend Keonna's door. I told my sister that I was going to sit on the porch for a while to get some fresh air. The truth is, I didn't want to be bothered. I had so much on my mind, and it felt cluttered. I had lost my virginity to someone I didn't know, my mother's husband snuck in my bedroom whenever he wanted and did what he wanted to me, and my mother didn't believe me. I felt like everyone was against Sherri.

They knew right from wrong, but that didn't stop them. After sitting outside for a while, my sister told me to come in because it was getting dark outside. Moosewood wasn't a safe place to be at night. My sister and her friend sat in the kitchen listening to music while playing spades and gin rummy. I was so bored that I dozed off on Keonna's couch.

Keonna's door opened, and two men were talking, which immediately woke me up. I cracked my eyes open, only to see a dark-skinned guy and another guy. I couldn't quite see the other guy's face because he stepped back outside. The dark-skinned guy walked into the kitchen where my sister and her friend were. The other guy came in the house seconds later, and I'll be damned if it wasn't Mike. You would've thought he saw a ghost when he saw me sitting on the couch.

My sister came out of the kitchen and introduced the dark-skinned guy and Mike to me. Come to find out, Mike was Keonna's man. That's when I learned he was twenty-four years old. I felt guilty, embarrassed, and scared as shit at the same time. I wasn't scared of Keonna because I feared no one; I was scared of what would happen if my sister found out her friend's fiancé took her little sister's virginity.

Mike played everything normal the whole night, but I could tell that he was on edge.

Hours passed before we finally went home. Soon as we walked in the house, I went straight to my room and cried myself to sleep.

THE NEXT MORNING

I woke up and took a hot shower. When I was done, I packed the rest of my clothes. I had a couple of days left before it was time for me to go back to the pits of hell. The last thing I wanted to do was go back to Atlanta, but I didn't have a choice. I hated it there. It really wasn't Atlanta that I hated; it was the people in it. I begged my sister and father to let me stay. They told me I could, but of course, my mother told them no. I was going to miss my sister and my niece Ravine.

My sister took me to see my brother and other family members. I hadn't seen Donnie since I had been in Atlanta. He worked so much that he barely was at home with his own family. Donnie was happy to see me. We talked and laughed for hours.

After that, I went to stay a couple of nights at my father's house. I remember being in the room with Ma (stepmother), and she asked me why my hands were shaking. I didn't notice they were shaking until she said something.

"Is everything okay?" Ma asked me.

"I guess."

"You're too young to have bad nerves, Sherri," she said as she took a pull from her cigarette and stared at me. "Is somebody touching you?"

When she said that, I was shocked. I was trying to figure out how she knew.

"Yes, my mother's husband be molesting me every night almost."

"Oh, hell, nah. You mean to tell me a grown man be touching you every night? I will kill that motherfucker and cut his dick off. Don't no grown ass man have any damn business touching a little girl. Dan!" Ma yelled my father's name at the top of her lungs.

"Ma, please don't tell Daddy, or my mama will stop me from coming to visit."

"I don't give a damn about that. Dan!" Ma called my father's name again. She searched the house, but my father was gone.

She talked to me, hugged me, and told me everything was going to be alright. That was the best hug I ever had from a mother. All I wanted was somebody to believe me and listen to me. My own mother couldn't even recognize that I was being molested, but another woman could. I started to believe that my mother knew what Patrick was doing to me, but she just didn't want to acknowledge it.

It was finally time for me to go to that hell called home. I didn't want to leave my family, but I had no choice. I cried all the way to the Greyhound station. My sister thought I was crying because I had to leave, but I was crying because I knew I was about to be molested again.

THE NEXT MONTH, I DIDN'T GET MY PERIOD. I DIDN'T EVEN bother to tell my mother I missed my period because she probably wouldn't care anyway. Months passed, and I finally decided to tell my counselor at school that I had missed several periods and thought I was pregnant. I only told her because I wanted her to break the news to my mama.

When my mother found out, she was disappointed, but she didn't take it as bad as I thought she would. She couldn't be mad that I was pregnant anyway. If her man wasn't molesting me every night and exposing me to things that I shouldn't experience, this probably would've never happened. I was vulnerable, broken, and used to being taken advantage of. I was a little girl crying out for help, love, and protection. Nobody cared what I was going through but me.

When I got home from school, Bonnie took me to take a test at the doctor. She kept asking me who the father was. I knew deep in my heart that my mother thought Patrick was the father. When I told her it was Mike's baby, she called to tell my sister. That caused chaos, of course, because my sister had to tell her friend that her thirteen-year-old sister was pregnant by her fiancé.

My sister was livid, and she was ready to whoop Mike's ass. Chelly felt that Mike took advantage of me because my sister had been telling them what Patrick had been doing to me. I told my sister about the situation a couple of times, but I made her promise not to tell Bonnie. I told my sister that if she said something, I would never see them again, and she promised she wouldn't tell.

My mother wanted to press rape charges on Mike because of his age. I told my mother not to do it. Although he was older than me, I didn't feel like he raped me because I agreed to do it. I didn't understand how it was so easy for my mother to press charges on another man but wouldn't press charges on the man who was coming into my room every night and assaulting me. My mother was asshole backward, and she knew it.

I only had five and a half months before I was due to give birth, and I was terrified as heck. At only thirteen years old, I was pregnant. I didn't know anything about taking care of a baby. Hell, I barely knew how to take care of my damn self. I thought about getting an abortion, but it was too late. Plus, my mother didn't believe in abortions anyway. I bet if it was Patrick's baby, she would've made me get one.

My cousin, Nate, had come from Mississippi to live with us for a while. Nate was one of my favorite cousins on my mother's side. I was happy he was there because I knew it would stop Patrick from coming into my room every night. God had finally sent someone to protect me from everything that was happening to me, at least I thought.

Chapter Seven
AVONDALE MALL

1997

One day I was at Avondale mall with my friends, and I noticed this tall guy checking me out. I ignored him because I wasn't interested in boys, especially after what I had been through. I felt like every boy was the same. All they wanted was one thing, and that was to take advantage of me. Plus, I was thirteen and pregnant. Who would want me, anyway?

I walked around the mall with my friends for a while until it was time for us to go. Before I could leave the mall, the dude who was checking me out by the food cart approached me. He was nice looking, and all the girls in the mall were trying to talk to him. If I didn't know any better, I would've thought he was a celebrity from the way the girls surrounded him. He stood about

6'3" with brown eyes and an athletic build. His haircut was low, with enough waves to make you seasick. He was dressed in a red jogging outfit with black gym shoes; I can't remember what kind. His facial hair and goatee were neatly trimmed.

"What's up, shawty? You cute."

"Hey," I said in my shy voice.

"Girl, he is cute," one of my friends whispered.

"Can I get your number?"

I hesitated for a second because, like I said before, I wasn't into boys, but I guess it was nothing wrong with a little conversation.

"Yeah, you can."

"What's your name?"

"Sherri, what's yours"

"Leon, how old are you?"

"Fifteen," I lied. I didn't know why I lied at the time, but I did.

"How old are you?"

"Seventeen."

"You sure about that?" I questioned.

The last man who told me he was seventeen turned out to be twenty-four.

"Yes, I'm sure. A lot of people think I'm older because of my facial hair." Leon reached in his pocket and showed me his ID.

I glanced at his birth date, and sure enough, he was seventeen years old. We talked for a while then exchanged numbers. After weeks of talking on the phone with Leon, we became very close. We spoke every day almost if he wasn't busy. After we had been friends for a while, he asked me to become his girl. I told him yes, I would love to.

Leon was different; he wasn't trying to have sex with me or force me to do anything I didn't want to do. It was conversation only. We would talk and laugh on the phone for hours. Lord knows I hadn't smiled or laughed in a long time. As Leon and I became closer, I started telling him the things that Patrick was doing to me. Leon begged me to come and live with him and his mother. I knew my mother wasn't having that, though.

Leon's mother, Ms. Tonya, was a paralegal, and she was super cool. She was very outspoken and didn't care if she hurt your feelings or not. That's what I liked about her. Ms. Tonya spoiled the shit out of Leon and his siblings. Although Leon was a teenager himself, his mother let him have his space. Leon hated Patrick, and he wanted him dead as bad as I did. The only thing that stopped him from killing Patrick was God and his mother.

Leon and I had a good relationship, but he was very overprotective. I remember going to see him one day. I had on a black skort, a white shirt, and some white wedges. He had a fit and made me put on this big ass red football jersey because he said I was showing too much. I thought that was cute. Leon was very possessive of me and didn't want anyone to look at me.

When I was with Leon, we always did typical teenage stuff like watch movies, talk, go swimming, or just chill. It was never about sex with him, and I loved that. I remember we had our first big argument because he found out I was pregnant. He swore up and down that I didn't tell him I was pregnant when I met him. I knew for a fact that I let him know I was pregnant when we first talked on the phone. I thought he was going to break up with me over the situation, but instead, we worked it out.

Leon was very supportive of my pregnancy. He made sure I had everything I needed, and he even gave me money to go shopping to buy baby stuff.

Two and a half months after being with Leon, we eventually had sex. We didn't have sex a lot because my mother barely let me leave the house. I felt protected when I was at his house. I could get some sleep and not worry about Patrick coming in while I was resting.

I was in love with Leon, at least I thought I was until things started to take a turn for the worse. I know you're wondering what a thirteen-year-old sexually abused girl knows about love or a relationship. The answer is, I didn't know shit. I guess I was a little girl searching for love in all the wrong places.

I was depressed, vulnerable, and my self-esteem was low. Although I was beautiful, I damn sure didn't feel like it. All I wanted was to be loved by my mother and my so-called stepfather. I didn't understand what I did to deserve this type of treatment; I just wanted to be a normal child for God's sake, but Patrick took that away from me at an early age. I didn't get to experience being a child because I was too busy being molested every night.

I was thirteen and pregnant. You know how embarrassing that shit is as a child? I don't think you do. Kids were laughing at me, and I was called every name you could possibly think of. The children who were bashing me didn't know my story, but I bet if they did, they would've been a little nicer. There was time I wanted to kill myself to get rid of the pain, but I couldn't. I even told my mother that I wanted to kill myself. She told me I was going straight to hell because killing yourself is a sin. The part that hurts me the most is that my mother wouldn't believe or protect me. As many times as I told her, you would've thought she would take some type of action, but she didn't.

What I thought was love was really puppy love. In the beginning, things were good, but in the blink of an eye, things went wrong. Some days, I would call Leon, and I wouldn't get an answer. I would call his friends, and they would tell me they hadn't talked to him. I knew they were lying because Leon never went a day without talking to his boys. This was the first time I experienced a woman's intuition. I knew in my heart it was somebody else, but I tried my best to ignore it.

Eventually, Leon would return my call and tell me a pack of lies. He would say things like, "I was at work, and I didn't hear my pager go off," or "I was sleep. I just woke up." That was his favorite line. I told Leon that if I found out he was cheating on me I would leave him for good.

One day, the truth finally came out when he got busted with some chick named Karen. The crazy part is his ex-girlfriend called and told me everything. I guess his ex was mad because he wasn't with her anymore. She even gave me the address to where he was. I caught the bus to the address, and I'll be damned if one of his boys didn't answer the door.

"Where Leon at?" I asked, barging into the house.

"I don't know. He's not here," his boy replied.

"He's with my friend, Karen, why?" a girl said.

"Where does Karen live?"

"None of your business," the girl replied.

"Jay, where is Leon?" I asked his friend. He shrugged. "Tone, where is Leon since Jay is acting dumbfounded?" I asked his other friend.

"I don't know."

I look over at Jay, and he was whispering on the house phone. I knew in my heart that he was talking to Leon's stupid ass.

"I will take you to where Leon is," the girl said with a grin on her face.

"Okay."

I knew the girl was up to something, but I wasn't scared of shit. I had so much animosity built up inside me, and I didn't think anyone wanted to mess with me.

"No, the hell you won't," Jay shouted. "You're not taking her nowhere."

"Why not?"

"You know why."

Jay grabbed my arm and took me outside. "Look, you have to leave, okay. Leon doesn't want anything to happen to you. Just know he loves you."

"If he loves me, where is he?"

"Sherri, just leave, okay. I will walk you to the bus stop."

My heart was crushed. I couldn't believe Leon was treating me like this. The boy who I thought loved me and would never hurt me was playing me. I guess the saying, *niggas ain't shit*, is true. The whole bus ride home, I cried my eyes out. I kept asking myself what I did wrong to deserve this type of hurt.

Hours later, Leon called me, and we had a bad argument.

"You really would hurt me, Leon, when you know what I go through at home?"

"How did I hurt you, Sherri?"

"You cheated on me."

"No, I didn't."

"Yes, you did. Your ex-girlfriend, Teonna, already told me the truth.

"Fuck that bitch! She wasn't saying that when she put honey on my dick and sucked it. Did she tell you that?"

When he said that, I had no more words for him. I hung my house phone up and turned the ringer off. Not only was he cheating with Karen, but he'd also just admitted to letting his ex-girlfriend suck him up. To make matters worse, I found out that Leon was a stripper. I was pissed when I found that out. I asked Leon about it, and he admitted that he was. I cried my eyes out that night.

That same night, Patrick came to my room, kissing and sucking on my breasts. I was already hurt from what Leon did to me, and Patrick's perverted ass didn't make it any better. I didn't eat or sleep for days and cried until I couldn't cry anymore. What Leon did was devastating to me. I was no longer interested in him, and that was on my mama.

Leon blew my pager and house phone up for weeks. I ignored him for a while, and when I finally decided to answer, I told him it was over. In my eyes, we were broken up, but in his eyes, we were still together. Although we were broken up, that didn't stop him from being there for me. He made sure I was going to my doctor's appointments and getting the proper care. Leon made sure he checked on me every day and told me he loved me. One thing I could say is he still had my back and treated me like I was carrying his child.

I began to get even more depressed, not because we were broken up but because things got worse in my household. Patrick was now ramming not one but two and three fingers inside my vagina like it was his penis. It was the most uncomfortable feeling in the world, especially since I was pregnant. While his fingers were inside of me, he would suck and lick all over my breasts, or he would play with my clitoris. I was so disgusted that I could've vomited in his face. I wanted him to burn in hell with gasoline draws on, and I didn't care if my mother joined him.

Once again, I told Bonnie about Patrick coming into my room and touching me. My mother told me I was lying like always. I was so numb that those words didn't even hurt anymore. I got to the point that I didn't care about telling Bonnie.

Chapter Eight

1998

I was having stomach pains, and my mother rushed me to Grady Memorial Hospital. They told my mother that I had dilated, but it was too early for me to give birth. Keep in mind, we didn't know how far along I really was since I waited months to tell her I was pregnant. They gave me so many different due dates, and we didn't know which one was correct. The nurse put an IV in my arm, then the doctor did a pap smear. When the doctor was done, she asked my mother if she could speak with her. I don't know what the doctor said to my mother, but she told them she was taking me out of the hospital.

The nurse took my IV out, and I got dressed.

"Ms. Bonnie, I don't think it's a good idea for you to take her out of this hospital," the doctor said.

"You're not about to stick no needle in her stomach. What if it pokes my grandbaby in the head or something? Sherri, come on, let's go," Bonnie stated.

The doctor and Bonnie had a couple more words, and then we left.

Days later

Bonnie and I had been out all day, and I was exhausted. When I got home, I went straight to my room to lie down because my pregnancy was wearing me out. I chilled and talked to my cousin, Nate, for a while until he fell asleep. Nate and I slept in the same room but in separate twin-sized beds. I didn't mind sharing my room with him because he was always at work or over his girlfriend Lisa's house anyway.

Nate's girl was cool, and I loved her like a big sister. Some days, Nate would let me go with him to her house when Bonnie allowed me to. Lisa and I became very close over time. Although my cousin was in a relationship, he had a big crush on my friend, Tashay, and Bonnie's friend's daughter Porcha. Tashay wasn't really interested in him, but Porcha was.

Nate and Porcha began dating while he was still with Lisa. I told him if Lisa ever found out, she would kill him, but he didn't care. My cousin wanted to have his cake and eat it too. Porcha fell madly in love with Nate, and months after they started to date, she found out about Lisa. Porcha cried for days, and I felt so bad for her. Nate was salty that he got caught, but it didn't stop him from being a player.

I lay in my bed, staring at the ceiling. Nate was knocked out with his Walkman playing music. It wasn't easy for me to fall asleep because I was too busy watching my door like always. Although Nate was there, I still didn't trust Patrick.

Soon as I closed my eyes, I felt my shorts and panties being snatched down at the same time. I open my eyes and screamed, "Stop!"

Patrick ran out of my bedroom and into the other room. I looked over at my cousin, Nate, and he was knocked out. I pulled up my shorts and panties then walked into Bonnie's room. Patrick was lying in bed next to Bonnie, like he wasn't just in my room.

"Ma, somebody just pulled my panties and shorts down," I said with an attitude.

"It probably was Nate," Patrick replied.

"No, it wasn't. Nate is asleep. It probably was you," I snapped.

My mother looked at Patrick, then looked at me. I just knew she was about to cuss him out. She had to see him run from my room because my room was down the hall from hers.

"Sherri, go back to bed," Bonnie told me.

"I hate it here," I said under my breath as I stormed into my room.

I could've told her I saw Patrick running out of my room, but what good would it have done? All she would do was believe his lies anyway. I knew my mother saw Patrick run his ugly ass into her room, and I knew she heard me say stop too. That night, I thought about setting the house on fire and praying that they died. The only reason I didn't was that Nate was there.

I went back to my room and lay in my bed with tears in my eyes. All night, I tossed and turned until I felt something wet going down my leg. I quickly woke up and felt between my legs. That's when I noticed my water had broken. I went into my mother's room to tell her my water had broken. Bonnie checked between my legs to make sure then told me it was time to go.

My mother and Patrick rushed me to Northside Hospital. My mother was in the room with me the whole time, but I told her that I didn't want Patrick in there while I was giving birth to my daughter. I wasn't at the hospital twenty minutes before I was in pain. I kept telling my mother that I had to doo-doo, and she kept saying, "No, you don't. It's only pressure from the baby."

I honestly didn't know if it was pressure or not. All I knew was it felt like I had to shit.

My mother walked with me into the bathroom and

stood in the door until I was finished. When I was done, I started bleeding.

"Oh my God, you're bleeding. That's the baby!" my mother shouted.

My mother helped me back to my bed. I was in so much pain; it felt like I was about to pass out.

"Mom, it hurts. It feels heavy down there," I told her.

"It's the baby trying to come."

My mother called for the doctor.

The nurses and doctor came rushing in. I'll be damned if Patrick wasn't right behind them.

I was in so much pain that I couldn't even tell Bonnie to make him get out. The only thing I was focused on was pushing my baby girl out of me. What woman in their right mind would want her husband to watch her daughter give birth? My vagina was exposed, and she didn't even care.

"Push," the doctor shouted.

"I can't!" I screamed.

It was hurting so bad that I kept closing my legs. The doctors, nurses, my mother, and Patrick were holding my legs open. I hated that Patrick was looking at me and touching me.

"You are going to smash the baby's head if you don't open your legs and push, Sherri. I need you to take a deep breath, open your legs, and push," the doctor stated.

I followed the doctor's directions, and minutes later, I gave birth to my baby girl. She was so cute, with the deepest dimples, and a head full of hair. She looked just like me, and I was so excited to meet her. I called Leon to let him know that she was here. He told me that he would come to see me tomorrow because he had to work.

Later that night, Leon and I debated on the phone for hours on what to name my baby girl. At first, he wanted to name her Fantasia, but I didn't like that name. I wanted to name her Sherriona, but Leon didn't like that. After brainstorming for a while, Leon came up with the cutest name, Davonna Monae, and I agreed to it. Davonna Monae Neal is my baby's full name. I call her Day-Day for short.

The next day, Leon came up to the hospital with balloons and a card. He kissed me on the cheek and took a seat beside me.

"How are you feeling?" he asked.

"Better."

"Where my baby at? I want to see her."

Although Day-Day wasn't his, you couldn't tell Leon that.

Soon as I was about to call the nurse, she walked in. She stood about 5'4" with brown skin, and her hair was cut short. Overall, she was a cute girl with a nice shape to match. I asked the nurse if she could get my baby for

Chapter Nine

THE DAY MY MOTHER'S HUSBAND BECAME MY RAPIST

Three to Four Months Later

When I was fourteen years old, we lived in some apartments off Memorial Drive. I can't remember the name of them; I just recall that I didn't know anyone over there. Bonnie and Patrick moved so much that it was hard for me to make friends. We moved at least seven to eight times in six years.

I used to always wonder why they moved so much. Patrick was probably molesting other girls in the neighborhood, and he made us move, so he wouldn't get caught. He was known for molesting little girls, and from what I learned, I wasn't the first one. As time went on, I found out he molested his first cousin, his sister, and some girls in Mississippi. He even touched a girl's breasts who I went to school with. I also learned that

Patrick wasn't allowed around his own daughter because he molested and raped some people his baby mother knew. Let Bonnie and Patrick tell it, it's all a lie, though.

Anyway, one day I was lying in my bed with Day-Day next to me. She had kept me up all night crying, and I was so tired. After I got her to go to sleep, I finally fell asleep myself. I remember lying on my stomach, and that's when I felt my pants snatched down. A liquid was then poured on my butt and between my legs. Next thing I knew, Patrick laid on top of me and rammed his penis into me.

I couldn't fight back because he was lying on my back while he raped me. Tears ran down my face as I looked at my baby girl sleeping beside me. The whole time, I prayed that he would stop, but he wouldn't. In my mind, I thought he was going to rape my daughter next. I was praying and wishing that my cousin Nate would walk in from his girlfriend's house and catch him. The whole time, I lay there with my eyes closed except for when I glanced over at my daughter.

When Patrick was done raping me, he ejaculated all over my butt. He whispered in my ear, "I know you're not sleep," then he got up and left my room.

Minutes later, I heard Patrick leave the house. Tears streamed down my face as I looked out the window to make sure his van was gone. I called Bonnie's job, but they said she already left for the day. I knew she was probably outside, waiting for Patrick to pull up. Instead of being on time to pick her up, he was raping me. I found a pen and piece a paper then wrote a letter to Bonnie, something quick and straightforward.

Mom, please don't let Patrick see this. He raped me while you were at work, and that's why he was late picking you up. Please don't let him see this.

I folded the letter then stuck it in my bra. Then I went into the bathroom and washed up. While I waited for my mother to get home, I called my friend, Tashay, to tell her what happened. She was crying her eyes out. I told her to tell her mother for me. Tashay and I had been hanging super tight for the last two years. Patrick tried to keep us away from each other, but he couldn't.

About forty-five minutes later, my mother and Patrick came through the door. I acted like I was still asleep until I felt like Patrick wasn't around. I peeked out my door and looked to the left. My mother was standing at her bed, folding clothes. I looked down the hall to my right and saw Patrick in the living room watching TV. With the letter in my hand, I ran as quickly as I could to my mother's room.

"Here, Ma, read this, and please don't let Patrick see it."

My mother took the letter and stuck it in her bra. I stood there for at least five minutes, waiting for her to read it. Finally, my mother walked into the bathroom that was in her room. When she came back out, her face was red as hell; I knew she had read my letter. My mother went back to folding clothes as if nothing happened.

Minutes later, I saw Patrick look down the hall. When he saw me standing next to my mama, he rushed into the room and picked up a Kmart ad off the bed.

"Bonnie, we should get Sherri this TV right here and this Sega game. Sherri, you want this?"

My mother nor I responded. Patrick was making himself look guilty, and he didn't even know it. My mother glanced at him and went back to folding her clothes. Bonnie was fighting back tears, but eventually, they began to fall.

"What's wrong with you, Bonnie?" Patrick nervously asked.

My mother walked out and went into the living room. The next thing I knew, they were arguing.

"Sherri said you raped her."

"I didn't touch that girl. She is lying. She just made that up because I don't give her what she wants."

"Why would she say something like that?"

"I don't know. Ask her."

I don't know what else Bonnie said to Patrick because she started talking low.

"The devil made me do it, Bonnie!" Patrick yelled.

"The devil didn't make you do no stuff like that."

"I promise, Bonnie, the devil made me do it. The devil made me do it!" he shouted.

When Patrick said the devil made him do it, he basically admitted to Bonnie that he raped me. Although he didn't come out and say, "I raped her," he still admitted it when he said the devil made him do it.

I was so happy that my mother finally heard the truth from her perverted ass husband's mouth. It had been six depressing, miserable ass years, and it was finally over, I told myself. Bonnie and Patrick argued for so long that I fell asleep. When I woke the next morning, I prayed that Bonnie had made Patrick pack his shit and leave. I was wrong; he was still there, and they were acting like everything was back to normal.

My mother told me to put Day-Day and me on some clothes because we were about to go somewhere. The first thing I thought was that she was about to take me to the doctor, but that didn't happen. Instead, we went somewhere else. Bonnie had the nerve to bring Patrick with us. I started making plans to run away with my baby because I refused to get raped again.

When we arrived back home, our apartment building was swarmed by cops. Patrick hopped out of his van and ran to the building when he saw the police holding my cousin, Nate, against the wall.

"I didn't do anything, sir. My name isn't Patrick. It's Nate Williams," I heard my cousin tell one of the officers. The driver and passenger windows were down, so I was able to hear everything.

"Who are you?" I heard an officer ask Patrick as he approached the building.

"I live here. That's my wife's nephew. What did he do?"

"What's your name, sir?" the detective asked.

"Patrick."

"Patrick Payne?"

"Yeah, that's me."

"Let him go," the detective told the officer who had Nate pinned against the wall.

At that point, my mother had hopped out of the car to see what was going on. The detective told my mother that he was there about a rape charge. I could hear the detective and Patrick having words. Patrick kept yelling, "I know my rights, and you don't have the right to arrest me."

I guess Patrick did know his rights because the detective didn't arrest him.

"Where is Sherri?" the detective asked.

"She's in the van. What you want to talk to her for?" he asked.

"Because we got a call that she got raped by you, sir," the detective said as he made his way toward the van.

"Are you Sherri Neal?" he asked as he slid the van door back.

"Yes."

"I need you to come with me," he stated.

"You can't question her. She's a minor!" Patrick shouted.

"The hell I can't."

The detective helped me out of the van and walked me to his car. He then opened the back door and told me to get in.

"Let her out of this car. She is a minor, and you have no right to question her," Patrick repeated.

"Sir, you are acting guilty right now. If you don't let me do my job, I will have you arrested," the detective said right before he got in his car.

He pulled off, and we were on our way. Minutes later, a horn began to blow from behind us.

"This man just doesn't stop, does he?" the detective stated as glanced in his rearview.

I looked back, only to see Patrick following us. We pulled over, and the detective got out of the car.

"Sir, if you don't stop following us, I will have you arrested for obstruction of justice," he yelled.

"Her baby is crying. Her baby needs her," I heard Patrick yell.

"Sir, if you don't leave now, I will have you arrested."

"She needs to take care of her baby. Her baby keeps crying."

"You know what? Give me the baby!" The detective took the car seat and grabbed the baby bag.

"Now, if you follow me again, you will go to jail,

sir." The detective put Day-Day in the back seat with me then pulled off.

I was so happy that he got my baby away from Patrick. I was worried about what he would do to my baby while I wasn't around.

♥

WHEN WE ARRIVED AT THE STATION, I REMEMBER GOING into a room with a desk. The detective told me to take a seat. He pulled out a camera stand then set the video camera on top of it. When he turned on the video camera, I remember a red light coming on. He asked me to state my name then asked me what happened the day Patrick raped me. After that, he asked me tons of other questions.

When the detective was done interviewing me, he told me that I wasn't going back home. I remember the detective taking me to a place with a lot of beds in the room. Some kids were in there sleeping, so I assumed it was a shelter for kids. The detective showed me to the bed that Day-Day and I would sleep in.

"Everything is going to be okay, Sherri," he said then walked away.

I felt so scared and alone, surrounded by complete strangers. I was crying and praying that everything would be over soon. As I lay in bed, I pulled Day-Day close to me to make sure she was safe and warm. I cried until I finally fell asleep.

The next morning, I was awakened and told that I was being moved to a foster home. I grabbed me and Day-Day's belongings, then we left. I was nervous because I had never been in a foster home before. Although I didn't want to go, I had no choice. Plus, I had to do what was best for my baby and me.

When we arrived at the foster home, I was greeted by my foster mom. She stood about 5'3" to 5'5", and she had a caramel complexion. Her hair was gray and cut into a short hairstyle. My foster mom asked me some questions then showed me where I would sleep. Ms. Brown told me she had a five-hundred-dollar voucher for me, so I could go shopping for me and Day Day. The girls in the foster home were cool. They all loved Day-Day and wanted to hold her.

That same day, my foster mother told me that they had to separate Davonna and me, and that's when my world came crashing down. Ms. Brown told me that kids Davonna's age weren't allowed to stay at the foster home we were in, and she had to go to another home. Tears fell down my face. I was speechless and didn't know what I was going to do without my baby. I didn't trust anyone with her because I felt like no one could protect her the way I did.

"Please don't take my baby away."

"We don't have a choice. She won't leave today,

though. We're still looking for a home for her, and that usually takes a week or two."

"Okay," I said with my head down.

I was sad that the only person I had to love me would be taken away.

THE NEXT DAY

My foster mom took me to the hospital to get checked out. After she signed me in, she told me she would be back soon then left. The doctor called my name, and I picked the car seat up with Day-Day in it and trailed behind her. She told me that she was going to perform a rape kit on me.

"Have you taken a shower or bath?" the nurse asked.

"Yes, I took a shower."

"When was this?"

"The day my mama's husband raped me."

"Why did you take a shower?"

"Because he ejaculated on me."

"Nine times out of ten, you washed the evidence away, but I'm still going to do one."

The doctor told me to get dressed from the waist down. She pulled out a metal comb and began to comb my pubic hairs. When I say that shit hurt like hell, believe me. I was crying and fighting through the pain at the same time; I couldn't wait for it to be over.

When the doctor was done, I waited for my foster mother to come. The whole time, I was debating if I wanted to run away or not. That was my only chance to keep my baby from being taken. The only problem was, I didn't have any money to get on the bus or call my friends. I knew I had to make a choice before my foster mom pulled back up to the hospital.

Time was running out, and I had to think quickly. That's when I saw a dude who Patrick's sister, Marquita, used to mess with named Red. I asked him to give me some bus fare, so I could get to my next destination.

"How did you get here?"

"My foster mom. I was put in foster care because Marquita's brother, Patrick, raped me. Now they're trying to take my baby away from me."

Red eyes grew big when I told him that. "Okay, I will help you. You can get on the bus with me. We got to hurry up because it will be pulling up any minute now."

Red grabbed the car seat, and I threw the baby bag over my shoulder. We speed-walked to the bus stop, and as soon as we got there, the bus pulled up. If we would've been ten seconds later, we would've missed it. The bus ride to the train station wasn't that long, but it seemed like forever to me. I was so paranoid that I was looking out the window every chance I got to make sure we weren't being followed.

We got off the bus, and Red told me he couldn't help me anymore, and I was on my own from here. He handed me Day-Day, and I took a seat on the bench. I didn't know where I was going. I started to think that maybe I made a mistake by running away, but what else was I supposed to do? I couldn't let them take my baby away. What if I never got to see her again? What if my mother tried to get her? What if she got molested and raped? What if she grew up not knowing me? All those questions were racing through my mind, and I just wanted this nightmare to be over.

I walked to the payphone and called Bonnie's friend, Nina, collect. Thank God she accepted my call. I told Ms. Nina what was going on, and she told me she was on her way to pick me up.

"I talked to your mom. She said the police have been watching her house."

"For real?"

"Yes. So, you can't go back there."

"Where I'm going to go?"

"You can stay at my house until we figure it out."

When we got to Ms. Nina's house, she called my mom and put me on the phone. I didn't know what to say to her. The words I wanted to say, I couldn't.

"Hey, this ReRe," I said, using a nickname I made up just in case her phone was tapped.

"Hey. Why you tell them people Patrick raped you?"

"Because he did."

"No, he didn't. You can't come back to my house because the police are watching. Patrick ran when they tried to arrest him. They sit outside in that van, looking at that newspaper like I don't know they cops, and it's your fault. I called your sister, Chelly, so she can come get you and take you back to Cincinnati because, like I said, you can't come here."

Tears filled my eyes. "Okay," I said, then hung up.

Instead of my mother taking me back in, she left me out. Bonnie still believed her husband over me. She didn't have any concerns about my wellbeing. All she was worried about was getting me to Cincinnati, so I could be out of her hair. Bonnie didn't care that her baby girl got raped by her husband. She didn't care that my baby and I were homeless. All she cared about was that no good ass child molesting, raping husband of hers. I couldn't wait until he went to jail and rot in hell. I prayed that the men in prison would rape his ass, just like he did me.

Days later, my sister, Chelly, arrived in Atlanta to pick me up. I was so happy to see my sister that I didn't know what to do.

"I got to meet Mom at the store to pick up this money. I want you to stay in the car because I don't know if Mama is being followed," Chelly told me.

"Okay."

We pulled up to the store minutes later. My sister went in, grabbed the money, then made her way back to the car. The whole ride to Cincinnati, all I kept thinking about was why my mother didn't believe me. What was it going to take for her to open her eyes and see Patrick for the monster he is? I was a little girl scorned, and my heart was as cold as ice.

From the age of eight to fourteen, I was felt on like a grown ass woman. Can you imagine getting your breasts sucked and your barely developed vagina fingered at eight years old until the age of fourteen? Then, at fourteen, you get raped. That was six years of non-stop torture. I can't even imagine a man doing something like that to my daughter. I know for a fact that I would be in jail for murder. The pain I went through, I wouldn't wish on nobody, not even my worst enemy. This is a lifetime of pain that doesn't go away when the situation is over because it's still embedded deep in your memory.

When I got to Cincinnati, I stayed with my dad, my stepmom, and my youngest stepbrother, Deon. We resided on the west side on Mustang Ave. My father and I had a talk about what Patrick did to me, and I could see his eyes tearing up. My father wasn't the type to show his emotions, but he did that day. He wanted to kill Patrick's ass, and who could blame him? My father called the detective to get information about the case, but he didn't answer, so he left a message. After that, he called Bonnie to talk to her.

Of course, Bonnie told my dad that Patrick didn't do any of the things I was saying. My father wasn't buying Bonnie's bullshit. He asked Bonnie when my court date was, and Bonnie gave him the information. Before hanging up, he told her that he will see her in court.

Weeks later, the detective told my daddy that he had been trying to get in touch with him because we missed the court date. My father informed the detective that Bonnie gave him a totally different date. He was pissed the fuck off, and he wanted to give Bonnie a piece of his mind. The detective told my dad that he would let him know about future dates.

Since my daddy had his own business to run, it was hard for him to keep in touch with law enforcement in Atlanta. The detective would call my father and leave messages on the house phone, but by the time someone checked the messages, it would be weeks later. My father would call the detective back, but he would be out of the office.

They were playing phone tag back and forth for weeks, sometimes months. After I missed so many court dates, they eventually threw the case out. My father apologized for missing my court dates, and he promised me that I would never have to go back to Atlanta. I was excited when my father told me that. Although I wanted Patrick in jail, I was happy to know that I didn't have to face his ugly, perverted ass. As long as my baby and I were safe, I didn't care about anything else.

A MONTH LATER

My father told me to get dressed, so he could take me to get enrolled in school. I slipped on some white pants, a plaid maroon and white shirt, and some black clogs. I pulled my long, thick, black hair into a ponytail and told my daddy I was ready.

My dad grabbed his coffee then we made our way out the door. Minutes later, we pulled up to Aiken High School. We walked into the office, and I took a seat in one of the chairs that were lined up against the wall. This girl rolled her eyes at me like she was jealous of me. I didn't like the vibe I was getting from ole girl at all. She just didn't know, I had so much anger built up in me that I would beat her senseless. Dudes were coming in and out of the office, and they were checking me out. I wasn't interested in any of their asses. All I was trying to do was get my education and be the best I could be for my daughter.

"Sir, do you have custody papers?" the lady asked my father.

"No, I don't. I don't have custody right now. I'm on the verge of getting custody."

"Well, she can't start school until we have documents proving you are her legal guardian."

"How am I supposed to get that?"

I could tell that my father was getting frustrated.

"You have to go to court, sir."

"Okay. Sherri, come on."

I threw my bookbag over my shoulder and trailed behind my father to his truck.

After months of staying with my father, he told me I had to stay with my sister for a while. I was happy because it was boring as heck at my dad's house. He and my stepmom were always at work, and my stepbrother was always outside with friends doing lord knows what.

Chapter Ten

*L*ife wasn't getting any better for me. In fact, it was getting harder by the day. I was a teenager with a baby, no income, and no education. It felt like my back was against the wall, and the world was on my shoulders. Although I had my family to help me, they had their own families to take care of. I was stressed out like a grown ass woman. I'm surprised I didn't have gray hair at a young age. All I wanted was to live a normal, teenage life, but it was too late for that. My adolescent life went out of the window when I gave birth to Davonna. I didn't know how it felt to go to prom or to the mall with my friends after school or how it felt to go to high school basketball and football games. I always wanted to be a cheerleader for football, but I never got to experience that.

Patrick and Bonnie had messed my life completely

up. I blamed them for everything that happened to me. At times, I used to wonder if I never got molested or raped how my life would be. The more I thought about it, the more I hated Patrick and Bonnie. All my mother had to do was believe me. Instead, she turned her back on me. How could a mother be so heartless and careless about something that was supposed to be precious to her? I could never be that cold hearted.

ONE DAY, SOMEONE TOLD ME ABOUT A PLACE IN CLIFTON, Ohio, that made fake IDs. That was my chance to get a job! All I needed was someone to buy the ID for me because I didn't have a dime to my name. I thought long and hard about the consequences of getting caught with a fake ID, but that didn't stop me from trying to get one. Finally, I decided to ask my sister to take me to get one, and she did with no hesitation. She understood that I had a baby to take care of, and I had to do what I had to do.

The fake ID wasn't what I expected at all. It looked nothing like a state ID. A blind man could see the shit wasn't real. It didn't even say state ID on it; it said identification card. There was no way in hell I would get a job with that piece of shit, but that didn't stop me from trying. I made sure I put that I was eighteen years old on the ID. That way, I wouldn't need a work permit.

The next day, I caught the bus and put in several applications. Within days, I had my first interview at McDonald's. I was a nervous wreck walking into my interview. This was the first interview I'd ever had, and I didn't know what to expect.

After the manager asked me numerous questions, she told me I had the job. I was excited until she asked for my ID and social security card. I wasn't worried about my social because I knew it was legit. I was more concerned about this fake ass identification card that I was about to hand her. I grabbed my social and ID out my back pocket then gave it to her. She glanced at my social security card then the identification card.

"What kind of ID is this?" the manager questioned.

"Oh, it's an identification card. I lost my state ID, and this is all I have for now," I lied.

"I don't know if we can accept this," she said and glanced at the card again."

Minutes after scanning the card, she told me that she would go ahead and accept it, but I had to bring my state ID as soon as I got it.

"Okay, thank you," I told her, feeling relieved.

The manager gave me my orientation and training date, then I made my way home. I was so happy I got the job, and all I could do was thank God. Now I could finally take care of my daughter without depending on my family.

I went home and told my sister the good news, and

she was happy for me. The next day, I went to my orientation and started working the day after that. A couple
of weeks later, I got my first check, but I had hell trying
to cash it. No bank or check cashing place wanted to
accept my identification card. I had to have my sister
deposit it in her account. The first thing I did with my
money was buy pampers, wipes, and clothes for
Davonna. I wanted to make sure she had everything she
needed so I wouldn't have to depend on anyone else. I
tried to enroll in GED classes so I could graduate, but I
had hell doing that because I was a minor.

AS TIME WENT ON, I WAS INTRODUCED TO A DUDE NAMED
Antonio Monroe. I was about fourteen and a half when I
met him, and he was seventeen. Someone I grew up
with gave him my number, and we started talking. We
talked on the phone for months before we saw each
other. The crazy part was, I loved Tonio and had never
met him a day in my life. I guess I was so eager to be
loved that I fell for anything and anybody. I was young,
vulnerable, and searching for love in all the wrong
places. I wanted to be loved so badly that I looked for it
in men.

The love I found in Tonio was the love I felt had been
missing from my life. He would listen to me, and he
cared about what I was going through. I had finally let

Antonio convince me to meet him in person for the first time. At first, I hesitated, but since it was my day off, I went. Plus, I was bored with nothing to do.

I was nervous about meeting Tonio because I didn't know how he looked, but it wasn't like I cared, because I already had deep feelings for him. I met up with Tonio, and let's just say his voice didn't match his looks. Have you ever heard somebody's voice on the phone, and they sounded good, but in person, they didn't look good? That was Antonio.

Don't get me wrong, he wasn't butt ugly, but he wasn't my type. He stood about 5'11" with dark skin and weighed about two hundred pounds of solid weight. He was built like the rapper, Fifty Cent, and he wore plats and braids sometimes. If you didn't know him, you would swear up and down he took steroids. That wasn't the case, though, he was just naturally built, and working out added to it.

Tonio and I became closer over time. Although he wasn't my type, he had a good sense of humor, and most of all, I felt protected. The only thing I didn't like about Antonio was that he was a drug dealer. He wasn't a kingpin or anything like that, but he had a little money. One thing I can say about him is he had a hustle hand to be seventeen years old. I would watch him flip a hundred dollars to a thousand quick. Tonio treated me well for the most part, but you know that shit changed in the blink of an eye.

Within weeks of meeting Antonio in person, I was getting into it with his ex-girlfriend Moe. He claimed she was his ex, but Moe was claiming something different. Moe told me that she and Tonio never stopped messing around, and he was at her house a couple of days ago. I asked Tonio several times if this was true, and of course, he told me no. I didn't let what Moe said faze me because there wasn't any proof that they messed around, and I knew females would sometimes say whatever because they were jealous.

After dating Tonio for a couple of years, I became pregnant with my son Quanterrious. I had my son at sixteen years old. I know you're probably wondering what the hell I was thinking. The truth is, I wasn't thinking; I was just blinded by love. I thought I had it all planned out. I wanted the family I never had.

For a while, I had been living back and forth between Antonio's mom and my dad's house. I felt like I was a burden on my sister because after I had stayed with her for a while, she started complaining. Everything I did was a problem, and I began to feel unwanted. I didn't know what the problem was because the majority of the time, I barricaded myself in my room.

Eventually, Chelly told me it wasn't me. She said that she had a lot on her mind. Come to find out, she was going through problems with her baby daddy because he was cheating on her. Not only that, but he left her for another woman. I couldn't even imagine what she was going through. However, I still gave my sister her space and stayed away. I would visit her and my niece, Ravine, from time to time.

Months later, my sister moved to Atlanta with my mom. I told her to make sure she watched after my niece because Patrick is a pervert. My sister knew what Patrick had done to me, but my mother had brainwashed her into not believing me. One thing my mother was good at was convincing people to believe her and Patrick's truth. The sad part is, she was too blind to see the truth in her own husband. Bonnie and Patrick are the true definitions of a wolf in sheep's clothing.

My mother had told my sister so many lies about me that she started to turn her against me. She made me out to be a liar and basically a hoe. Me having kids at a young age didn't make it any better. See, my sister was on the outside looking in, so of course, she was going to believe Bonnie's lying ass. What child wouldn't believe their mother? The difference between my sister and me is that she didn't go through sexual abuse. She had a good life. Chelly didn't have to worry about a man coming into her room every night because she lived with my father, and he would've killed his ass.

ANTONIO EVENTUALLY GOT HIS OWN PLACE IN THE FAY Apartments. I, along with Davonna and Quanterrious, moved in with him. As time went on, I began to see Antonio's true colors, and he definitely wasn't the man I met years ago, or should I say, boy. Tonio was caught cheating left and right. Every time I turned around a female was calling my phone. I can't even count on my fingers how many times he cheated because I don't have enough fingers or toes.

I tried to leave Tonio, but he became violent. He would hit me, choke me, and pull my hair. I couldn't believe that he was doing these things to me, especially knowing everything I had been through. One time, he beat me from the downstairs to the upstairs. There was blood all over the place. I remember my friend, Tia, coming to see me, and she began to cry when she saw blood everywhere. It was blood from the bottom of the stairs to the top and all over the bathroom floor.

All I wanted was out of this relationship, but it was so hard to leave. I didn't have anywhere to go. My father had a house full staying with him, and I didn't want to be a burden on him and my stepmom. My sister had moved to Atlanta, and I damn sure wasn't going to live with Bonnie and Patrick. I would've been in jail for murder, and that's a fact. The abuse, the lying, and the cheating were all becoming too much. I had enough trauma and hurt from my past, and now, here I was, dealing with emotional, mental, and physical abuse.

I still wasn't over what Patrick did to me; I just tried my best to bury it as deep as I could. Although I was still traumatized, I managed to smile and pretend like everything was okay. On many days, I wanted to kill myself and just get it over with. I would have if I didn't have kids. I'd be damned if Bonnie and Patrick's weird ass raised my kids. I could've stayed with my dad, but he already had a house full in his two-bedroom apartment.

For months, I dealt with domestic violence from Tonio. I tried to leave, but he would always fight me to stay. I didn't understand why Antonio wouldn't let me go. All he did was cheat and abuse me when he felt like it.

I remember when I was pregnant with Quanterrious, Antonio and I went to Atlanta, GA, to visit my friend Tashay. We weren't even at Tashay's mama's house a whole week before Tonio started cheating. Days later, I ended up going in labor while we were still in Atlanta. My sister and Bonnie met me at the hospital, and thirty minutes later, I was pushing.

After I had Quan, my mother and sister left because they had to go to work. I was shocked that Bonnie even came with my sister. I kept calling Tonio's phone, but he wasn't answering because he was too busy with that other chick. There I was in the Dekalb County hospital giving birth to his son while he lay up with some chick he didn't know. I called his phone several times, but he didn't answer. I texted him to let him know I was in labor then he popped up hours later.

When he got there, he tried to give me a kiss, and I told him not to touch me. Tonio's phone rang, and he answered it. I heard him tell whoever he was talking to that he was at the hospital with me. I assumed it was his mama or a family member until he told me that Vicky said congratulations. My blood began to boil, and my blood pressure shot through the roof. Vicky was an older chick who he got busted cheating with months ago.

"Are you really talking to that bitch while I'm right here?" I shouted.

I was mad that I was too sore to get out of the bed and smack his ape looking ass.

"I don't know what you mad for. This is just my friend," Tonio stated.

"You so disrespectful." I rolled my eyes as tears streamed down my face.

Minutes later, the nurse came in and checked my blood pressure.

"Are you okay? Your blood pressure is extremely high," the nurse said.

I nodded.

She knew I was lying because I was crying.

"If you're going to make her cry and upset her, you need to leave."

Tonio thought it was funny and walked out the door.

He couldn't even be a man and stay there to make sure I was okay after giving birth to his son.

After staying in the Fay Apartments for a while, our house got shot up. Some dudes that Antonio knew had broken into our home, and Antonio retaliated. He shot at one person, and while we were sleeping, they shot our house up. I packed my stuff and stayed at a friend's house for a couple of weeks. Tonio was mad that I left, but I had to protect me and mine. Antonio got evicted months later, and I was back staying with my dad for a while. My dad didn't care for Antonio because he'd heard about the things Antonio was doing to me. I don't know how he found out because I sure didn't tell him. When my dad would ask me if it was true, I would deny all allegations.

While staying with my dad, my relationship with Tonio got better. I guess we needed some time away from each other. We weren't fighting and arguing like we used to. We would talk on the phone every day all day. Antonio would come over to my dad's house and chill with me sometimes, but he was only allowed on the porch. Sometimes my stepmama would let him come in. I liked the space that Tonio and I were in. It felt like it did when we first met.

As time went on, I discovered that I was pregnant with my daughter, Makayla, at the age of seventeen. I had her at eighteen. I had promised myself that I wasn't having any more kids. Did I regret getting pregnant at a young age? Absolutely, but at the time, all I was thinking about was being loved unconditionally by my kids. I wanted to give my kids the type of love Bonnie should have given me. I didn't plan my pregnancies, they just happened.

♥

Soon as I turned eighteen, I got my first apartment in Winton Terrace. It was low income, but it was mine. It was decent; I just hated that I lived in the hood. When I first moved into my apartment, Antonio was locked up on a drug charge. He called and wrote to me every chance he got, telling me how he was going to become the best man I ever had. Tonio also told me he changed, and he wanted things to work out between us. The words he said melted my heart, and I believed him.

Months later, Antonio got out, and I must say we were doing good. Then he got caught cheating with an older, mixed chick named Mariah, who looked like an old ass granny. Most mixed people are beautiful, but she wasn't all that. Mariah put you in the mind of the lady who plays Rosanne from the TV sitcom. She had pretty hair, but that was about it. Mariah dressed like she fell in a Goodwill dumpster. Right after he got caught cheating, Tonio was back in jail again. I was happy, to be honest, because he was stressing me the hell out.

I stayed in my first apartment for about six months

until I saw a mouse in my house. Do you know this mouse had the nerve to climb up in my damn bed and watch me as I was writing a letter? I was scared as shit. I still laugh about that till this day. I called my daddy to come get me, and I never went back to that apartment again. Weeks later, I got a phone call from Ashwood Apartments, saying that I made it to the top of the waiting list, and I could come and look at my apartment.

A couple of weeks later, I moved into my new, three-bedroom two-bathroom apartment. The apartment went by our income, but it was in a nice neighborhood. My dad and my stepbrother, Deon, helped me move all my belongings in. My stepbrother lived there with me for a while.

Not long after I moved into Ashwood apartments, Tonio got out of jail, and like a fool, I took him back. Our relationship was going surprisingly well, but of course, you know he slipped up again. It got to the point that I wasn't having sex with Tonio because I was turned off by him. I didn't want him to hug me, kiss me, or touch me. Hell, I barely wanted him to look at me. Tonio would beg me to have sex with him, but I wouldn't.

I was sleeping on the couch one day, and Tonio woke me up to have sex. I told him no and fell back asleep. Minutes later, I felt warm liquid all over my face. This nigga had ejaculated on my face like I was some type of hoe. What kind of man would do this to the mother of his children?

I got up swinging. "You dirty bitch! Why would you do that to me?"

"Because you wouldn't give me none of that good pussy." He laughed.

I told him it was over and to get out. We had a big fight, but he wouldn't leave for anything in the world. Days later, he finally left. I didn't know what changed his mind, and I really didn't care. I was just relieved that he was gone. Don't get me wrong, it was hard for me when he left because I didn't prepare myself mentally, and not to mention I wasn't financially stable. I mean, I got a welfare check for $575.00 a month, but that was only enough to pay my bills. I had about $100 left after paying bills. I still had to buy things like clothes, household items, pads, and other stuff for the house.

I wasn't about to let that break me, though. I had to do what I had to do as a mother. Like Bonnie used to always say, God will make a way. If she didn't teach me anything else, she taught me that.

I WAS AN EIGHTEEN-YEAR-OLD SINGLE MOTHER WITH NO JOB or high school diploma. I had been in a relationship with Tonio for three years, and he took care of the kids and me, so I didn't have to work. He wasn't rich or nothing, but he had a little money. After we broke up, I didn't talk to him for days, and that was fine with me.

Antonio started blowing my phone up after a while. He was begging me to be back with him, but I kept telling him no. Did I want it to work out? Yes, because I didn't want my kids to grow up without both parents in the house. On the other hand, I was tired of being his fool, and I damn sure was tired of being his punching bag. I was tired of the arguing, fighting, lies, and cheating. I was stressed out, and I was too young for that, especially after what I went through in my childhood. I deserved happiness, and I was going to get it one way or another.

A month had gone by, and Antonio was still begging for us to be back together. He had promised me once again that this time would be different. I thought about it and decided to give him another try for the kids' sake.

I know what you are thinking, yeah, my dumb ass agreed to get back with him. Tonio told me before we got back together that he had something to tell me. He had the nerve to tell me he had another woman pregnant. My heart was crushed, and it felt like my breath left my body. Tonio had blown any chance he had with me. I wasn't about to be his fool anymore, and I definitely wasn't about to deal with another woman in the picture.

I told Antonio that I was done with him, and he might as well be with his new baby mama then hung up. Tonio blew my phone up for weeks, but I didn't answer. When I did finally answer, it was for the kids only. I went on with my life and started doing what was best for my kids and me.

I had been dealing with Tonio's shit from fourteen and a half years old until I was twenty. It was time for me to enjoy life to the fullest, and that's what I did. Tonio was hurt that I left him. He even threatened to kill me if I got another man. I didn't care about anything he was talking about.

After being broken up for a while, my mind was no longer on Tonio; I had moved on. It was the best decision I ever made in my life. I thought it would be hard, but it wasn't that bad. I cried some nights, but I eventually got over it.

Although Tonio and I were broken up, he did stay in the kids' lives for a while, but once I moved on for good, all that stopped. He didn't want anything to do with our kids. I guess the saying is true, mama's baby and daddy's maybe.

Chapter Eleven

I had become close with a girl named Nya when I first moved into Ashwood apartments. Nya didn't care for Tonio when we were together. She knew how he treated me, and always told me I deserved better. Some days when we would fight, I would hide over Nya's house to get away from Tonio.

Months later, a girl named Keke moved directly across the hall from me, and we became the best of friends. We instantly kicked it off when we met each other. Kee was cool, sweet, and laid back, just like me. She had a great personality and a heart of gold. Kee would give you the shirt off her back and shoes off her feet if you needed it.

Kee and I were together every day. If you saw her, nine times out of ten, you saw me. Kee was five years older than me, and she was on her grown woman shit.

She had just graduated from nail school, and she was a beast with the nails. That made me look up to her. Kee had one son, and that was my baby. I loved him like he was my own. We were more like cousins and sisters. Blood couldn't make us any closer. Kee was also having problems with her baby daddy at the time, and that made our bond even tighter.

Kee and I both enrolled in Southwestern College for the medical coding and billing program. They had a program where you could earn your GED and take your college courses at the same time. Since I didn't have my GED, that was best for me.

WE STARTED GOING OUT TO BARS AND CLUBS WITH KEE'S cousins. Before we went out, we made sure the kids were together, and we had all our college work done. The first time I experienced the club, I was in love. All types of men were showing me love. We weren't searching for love; all we wanted was to have a good time, and we did just that. Every Friday after college, we would go home, get dressed, then make our way to Motions Night Life. Neither Kee nor I drove, so we always rode with her cousins or my stepbrother Deon.

Motions was the place to be on Friday and Saturday nights. When we walked in, we turned heads. Men were on our ass like white on rice. The attention that those men were giving us was the attention we were looking for from our baby daddies. Tonio was pissed off when he found out I had started going out. He would blow up my phone and text me every five minutes. I didn't bother responding to him. I guess Tonio thought after a while I was going to give in, but it was over for that. He should've never let me get a taste of the world.

If I had known I was missing all this fun, I would've left his ass years sooner. I had all types of men trying to holler at me, including dope boys, business owners, security guards, college students, and motorcycle gang members. I loved the attention. I used to be at the club twerking my ass off. Although I didn't have an ass, I still knew how to make that thang shake. Sometimes after the club, Tonio would pop up at my house to see if I was with another man. He used to get on my nerves with that shit.

Months had passed since we broke up for good, and he was still on my ass. If he was on my ass like this when we were together, maybe we would have worked it out. Instead, he was busy chasing hoes, selling drugs, and getting locked up. While he was doing all that, I was preparing myself mentally to leave his sorry ass. Now that I was gone, he didn't know how to act. I even had to get my locks changed because he still had a copy of my key. Not to mention, he had kicked my door in once.

Anyway, every weekend, Kee and I partied. If we

SHERRI MARIE

weren't at the club, we were in the house with music blasting and a gallon of Seagram's gin. Sometimes we would have company, and sometimes it would be just us. Nya chilled with us a lot, but most of the time, she would be at home with one of her friends that she met off the chat line. Nya was the chat line queen. Most of the men she met on there, she didn't meet in person, but she did meet a few.

Nya used to always try to hook Kee and me up with her brothers, cousins, or friends. She met a dude named Corey off the chat line and fell in love with him. He would come to her house, but he never came alone; he always brought at least five to seven of his friends with him. Nya would beg for Kee and me to come over and chill with her. We did because we had nothing else to do. Our kids were either gone for the weekend or in the house sleep.

Since Nya, Kee, and I all lived on the same floor, we would go back and forth, checking on the kids to make sure they were still asleep. Nya had a daughter, but she was gone a lot on the weekends. She was either with Nya's mother or her sister. We would chill, drink, and talk shit all night with Cory and his boys. They were cool to be around and were all about having fun and not sex. Don't get me wrong, a couple of them liked Kee and me, but we kept it on a friendship level.

One day, Antonio popped up while we were chilling with Corey and his boys at Nya's house. Kee, my stepbrother Deon, and I were in the back talking while everyone else was in the living room socializing. Antonio was upset when he saw other men in the living room. That's when he did the unexpected. He cocked his gun and placed the cold steel against my forehead.

"Bitch, I will kill your ass."

"I can't let you do that, bruh. You going to have to kill me first," my stepbrother, Deon, said as he stood in front of me.

"Tonio, put the gun down!" Kee shouted.

Kee and my brother were trying to tell him to put the gun down, but it was going in one ear and out the other.

Nya heard the commotion and came to see what was going on. When she saw Antonio with the gun, she instantly called the police. I just knew he was about to take my brother's life then Kee and my life next. Finally, Tonio put the gun back on his waist then walked out of the bedroom.

My brother hugged me, and I returned the favor. Kee had tears in her eyes, and fear was written all over her face. I can't lie, my life flashed before my eyes, and all I could think about were my kids. I had so many things running through my mind at the time, and I couldn't keep up with my own thoughts. I didn't understand why Antonio was so mad when he was doing his thing with other women. I guess he hated the fact that I had moved on and was living life.

Chapter Twelve

Years Later

As time went on, I got involved in different relationships. It seemed like all men were the same, or I was choosing them wrong. One thing I can say is I didn't put up with half the bullshit I put up with from Tonio. Once they showed me who they really were, I was gone with no hesitation. I didn't care how long we were together and how much I loved that person. I refused to let another man hurt and abuse me. If Antonio didn't teach me anything else, I learned not to be a fool for these men out here. After what Antonio put me through, I was stronger but still damaged. Before I let a man walk over me like I was a doormat, I would be by myself, and that was a fact.

I got to a point in my life where I just didn't trust

anyone, not even myself. I started to drink heavily just to deal with the pain and feelings of loneliness. It seemed that everyone I trusted hurt me in some way. My mother, Patrick, Antonio, and other relationships that I had been in after Tonio had me messed up mentally and emotionally. What messed me up the most was being sexually abused for six years. I was looking for love in all the wrong places and letting men take advantage of me. All I wanted was to be loved, but instead, I got misused and mistreated. It was really messed up that I had to search for love in men at a young age. All I needed was two things, and that was to be loved and protected.

There is no way I should've had three kids by the age of eighteen, but I did. Do I regret having kids at such a young age? No, but I damn sure regret my baby daddies. If I could turn back the hands of time, and God gave me a chance to change one thing in my life, it would be my mother. The pain from being sexually abused lives with you forever. It isn't something you can erase out of your mind overnight. Sexual abuse stays with you for a lifetime, and it haunts you forever. No matter how deep it is buried, somehow, it always comes back to the surface. I could hear about somebody being sexually abused on the news, and it will make me have flashbacks of what happened to me.

People have a lot to say about those who have been sexually abused, but you can't judge unless you've been through it. I have been called all types of names, hoes, stupid, dumb, bitch, nasty, everything but the child of God. People used to say, "Dang, you're eighteen with three kids. You a hoe. My mama would beat my ass." My reply would be, "If you only walked a day in my shoes, I guarantee you would give my shoes back to me. I am a victim of molestation and rape! Until you walk in my shoes, don't speak on what you don't know."

People can judge all day, but they don't know your story. They don't know the hurt and pain that people face when dealing with sexual abuse. We might look happy on the outside, but deep inside, we're torn. We are hurting from all the pain and abuse we went through as a child. There is no professional help because no one cared enough. Even after I was removed from the situation, it still harmed me on the inside.

I want everybody reading this book right now to put yourself in my shoes. Imagine what I went through from eight years old to fourteen years old. Every night my mother's man coming into my room, digging his fat fingers into my immature vagina. I'm crying and pleading for him to stop but he wouldn't. He's sucking on my immature breasts and fingering me at the same time. Whispering in my ear, asking how it feels, and telling me if I play with my clitoris, it will make me feel good. Imagine telling your mother, but it falls on deaf ears, and the only person she believes is her husband.

Imagine going through that for six and a half straight

years with no help. Every day your vagina is sore. You're scared to pee because your poor vagina has been ripped open, and it burns like hell when urine comes out. Then, at the age of fourteen, your mother's husband comes into your bedroom and rapes you while your child is lying next to you. That was straight torture to me and my vagina. Can you imagine that? Hell nah, you can't!

So, the next time, you're ready to judge someone whose choices are not your own, take a moment to have some compassion. That girl you call a hoe might've been sexually abused. The stupid girl who always looks miserable might be going through domestic violence. That girl who got pregnant at twelve or fourteen years old might be getting raped every night by a family member. The girl who attempts suicide might be going through something so tremendously painful that death seems to be the only relief.

We never know what life has in store for us or what the next person is going through. Just remember to extend the same compassion to others that you would want for you or your own child. Why is that so hard?

Whew! I was in my feelings, but it needed to be said.

face looking ass was standing in the door. Kee and I spoke then took our bags into the guest room. Afterward, we went into the kitchen to find something to eat. Patrick and Howard were talking in the living for a while. When they were done talking, Howard came into the kitchen to talk to Kee and I. Patrick's big, thirsty, black, ugly self followed him. I rolled my eyes when I saw him coming.

Uncle Howard sat at the table, and Patrick joined him. I glanced over at Kee, and she grabbed the butcher knife off the counter and held it behind her back. I was engaged in a conversation with Uncle Howard when Patrick tried to grab me by my waist. Howard and Kee both looked at Patrick like he was crazy.

"Don't touch her," Kee said with an attitude, and her left eyebrow rose.

Patrick gave Kee an evil look, but what he didn't know was his life was on the line because Kee had that knife ready to stab his ass.

"I'm about to leave, but I will be back later to pick y'all up, so we can go somewhere," Howard told us.

We gave Uncle Howard a hug and walked him to his car.

"When you come back, I'm going to have them dressed up like little church girls. They going to have on the little skirts with the knee-high socks and bows in their hair," Patrick said as he stood in the door laughing.

I knew that perverted monkey hadn't changed.

Kee was ready to take his ass out, and he didn't even know it.

Patrick went into his room while Kee and I sat in the living room on the couch, directly across from each other, watching our soap opera *Passions*. Before we could even finish watching it, we were passed out. I don't know how long I was asleep, but I jumped up with the quickness when I realized where I was. I looked to my left, only to see Patrick sitting in the chair asleep with only his boxers on. For some reason, I felt like he was playing sleep. I looked over at Kee on the other couch, and she was passed out.

Please wake up, Kee. Wake up, please. God, please wake her up, I chanted in my head. Next thing I knew, Kee's eyes popped wide open. I looked at Kee then looked at Patrick.

"Let's go now," Kee said as she pointed her finger toward our guest room.

"What is wrong with him?" Kee asked as she pushed the door up. "If I have to kill him, I will."

"I told you he was a pervert, cuz," I said.

"I knew he was one when you told me your story, and I never doubted you, little cousin."

We still had two days left there, and I didn't know how we were going to cope. One thing for sure, I didn't trust Patrick's ass at all, and I was going to sleep with one eye open. Later that day, we got ourselves together so we could be ready when Uncle Howard came.

I didn't trust staying in the guest room by myself while Patrick was there, so I went into the bathroom with Kee. While Kee was in the shower, I did my hair, and while I was in the shower, Kee did her hair. When we were done, we went back to the guest room.

Uncle Howard called me and said he wasn't going to make it because something had come up. We were salty, but there was nothing we could do about it. For the rest of the night, we stayed in the guest room, chilling and laughing.

Next day

We got up, brushed our teeth, and sat in the living room watching TV.

"Let's go chill outside in the back, so I can roll up," Kee stated.

"Okay."

We made our way to the back porch, where we chilled, talked, and laughed for a while then went back inside.

As we sat in the living room watching TV, the pervert came into the living room with us, so we got up and made our way to the guest room.

"Why y'all keep isolating yourselves from me in my house?" Patrick shouted as he followed us.

"Whatever. We don't have to be around you if we

don't want to. You a grown ass man, why you want us in there with you?" I replied.

"Right," Kee agreed.

"This my damn house, and y'all trying to isolate yourselves from me. Sherri, you are acting differently since you around her!"

"I'm not acting like nothing. I grew up. I'm not that little girl no more."

"She isn't changing anything. We just don't want to be around you," Kee stated.

Patrick got upset and started walking toward Kee.

"I need you to back up and give me fifty feet," Kee shouted and punched her hand. "You aren't my mother-fucking daddy, so that means I will beat your ass. Now back up and give me fifty feet."

Patrick kept talking stuff, but he never got in Kee's face. I picked up my cell phone and called Bonnie.

"Hello."

"Ma, Patrick is over here picking an argument with us because he said we are isolating ourselves from him."

"That man is crazy. Let me talk to him."

All we kept hearing Patrick saying is, "They isolating themselves from me, Bonnie."

Not to mention he lied that we were smoking weed in the house. The messed-up part was I didn't even smoke weed. He must've smelled the weed on Kee's clothes when she walked past him. Patrick went on and on about us isolating ourselves from him. It was pointless calling Bonnie because he kept arguing with us.

My mother told us to go over Marquita's house until she got home.

Patrick used to always call Marquita a hoe and said he didn't want me around her. I would cry when I couldn't go to her house because I hated being at home with them. Marquita even stayed with us a couple of times, but not for long. Patrick used to always say that she was trifling and didn't like to clean after herself. So, she never lived with us for a long time.

Patrick didn't stop arguing with us when he hung up with Bonnie. I called Howard to let him know what was going on, so he could pick us up. He told us that he would come to get us shortly. Kee and I stood outside waiting for Uncle Howard because if would've stayed in the house any longer, we would've been on *The First 48*.

"You know I was going to kill him, right?" Kee said, referring to Patrick.

"I know you was, cousin."

"I was going to hit him right in the mouth with that barbell and fifty-pound weight."

"Girl, I don't have no bail money." I chuckled.

"I'm not going to jail in Snellville, GA. Bitch, I'm incompetent." We burst out laughing

"Patrick was about to get jumped, and that's a fact."

"On everything I love, he was," Kee replied.

Finally, Uncle Howard pulled up, and we left.

Twenty minutes later, we arrived at Marquita's house in the projects. Niggas were sitting on the roof and the hood of their cars with big bottles of Grey Goose. Soon as we got out of the car, they knew we were fresh meat. They were on us like white on rice, but Uncle Howard wasn't having that.

When we walked in, Aunt Marquita was cooking some ground beef. The house was trifling, and there were roaches everywhere. Kee and I didn't even want to sit down. Marquita offered us some of the nachos that she was cooking, but we declined. There was no way in hell I could eat with all those roaches around. Don't get me wrong, I lived in the projects, and I had been around roaches, but this was ridiculous. The entire time we were at Marquita's house, we sat outside. When it got dark, we decided to go in because niggas were acting crazy.

About an hour after we went into the house, my mother came to pick us up and take us back to her house. I didn't want to go back to her house, but we didn't have a choice, once again. We could've stayed at Quita's house, but I wasn't taking a chance on having a roach crawl in my ear.

❤

TRACY CALLED ME THE NEXT DAY AND TOLD ME SHE WAS ON her way to my mother's house. I didn't want her to come because Patrick was on some bull. Tracy was only getting dropped off because my mother was taking all of us to the Greyhound in the morning. When Tracy and her one-year-old son, Aries, arrived, I introduced her to my mama and ugly dude. After that, we went into the office to look up some houses. We all were planning to move down to Atlanta one day.

As we looked at houses, I noticed that Aries wasn't in the room anymore.

"Where is Aries?" I said to Kee and Tracy.

Tracy called his name, and he came running into the office where we were. We were all in shock when we saw that Aries' pamper was missing.

"What the hell?" Kee and I said at the same time.

"Where the fuck is my baby's pamper?" Tracy shouted.

Tracy immediately picked Aries up and began to check his body parts. This was the most embarrassing shit ever. I knew in my heart that Patrick had removed that pamper. Aries was around me all the time, and he had never taken his pamper off before. We were ready to kill Patrick's ass, especially Tracy. I just knew we were going to catch a case before we left Atlanta.

The three of us went back to the guest room to pack up our stuff, so we could leave the next morning. When we were done, we locked the door and lay in the queen-sized bed. Kee was on the left side of me, Aries and I were in the middle, and Tracy was on the right side. We talked about how perverted Patrick was and how we should kill his nasty ass.

After discussing what happened, we talked, laughed, and before I knew it, we passed out.

THE NEXT MORNING

The alarm went off, letting us know it was time to get ready to leave.

"Oh, my God!" Tracy shouted.

"What?" I asked as I looked over at Tracy.

"How my shirt got unbuttoned?" she questioned as she stared down at her exposed breasts. Tracy quickly started buttoning her shirt.

"Patrick perverted ass did it. I told you he was a molester and a rapist." I shook my head.

"Oh, hell nah, we got to get out of here before I kill his ass," Kee stated.

"You and me both," Tracy replied.

Bonnie was a damn lie when she said that Patrick had changed. The only thing that changed about him was his weight and his victims. We all got up and got ourselves together. When we were done, we put all our luggage in the car. I told my mother we were ready, and then we left. I was salty the whole time I was in Atlanta because I didn't see my sister or nieces. Come to find out, she ended up going out of town herself.

I was so happy to see the Greyhound station that I

didn't know what to do. I couldn't wait to get away from that perverted bastard. The messed-up part is that I was in my twenties, and Patrick still doing the same thing.

We got on the Greyhound and made our way back to Cincinnati. I was relieved to be out of their house. I couldn't believe what we had been through in the last couple of days. Not only was that shit embarrassing, but it was stressful. Bonnie was still blinded by Patrick's nonsense. My mother didn't see anything wrong with Patrick saying we were isolating ourselves from him. She didn't question herself on why her husband wanted those young, beautiful girls around him so badly. That disgusted me just thinking about it.

(Please keep reading because the story gets even deeper.)

Chapter Fourteen

Summer of 2004

$\mathcal{I}$ met Corey through a dude who Kee had started talking to named Tay. Tay had told Kee that he had somebody he wanted me to meet. I really wasn't interested in talking to anyone because I didn't have time for the games. I was focused on taking care of my kids and working. Tay asked Kee if it was cool for his boy, Corey, got my number, and I told her I didn't care. I didn't mind engaging in a conversation with Corey, especially when I was bored.

About an hour after Tay gave Corey the number, he called me. We had a good time on the phone, and I must say I was feeling his conversation. He was a cool person to talk to, and he kept the conversation interesting. Tay and Corey had made plans to hook up with us on the weekend. I was kind of anxious to see the man I had been talking to on the phone for the last couple of days. The weekend was only a couple of days away, but it felt like a lifetime.

Finally, the weekend had come, and it was time for me to meet Corey. Kee and I freshened up and waited for them to arrive. I was nervous about meeting Corey because I wasn't the type to do blind dates. Although it wasn't really a date, it felt like one. I had promised myself after the last dude I dealt with that I was done with these niggas. The last dude I was talking to named Juan was nothing but a liar. He lied so much; he will make you think the sun was blue when you know it's yellow. Juan was the true definition of a habitual liar. I left Juan alone with the quickness. Once he showed me his true colors, I showed him the door. I wasn't getting caught up with any more fuck boys.

After I put Juan out, I had to hide at Kee's house for months because he kept stalking me. Juan even tried to kick Kee's door down one day. She had to open the door and convince Juan that I wasn't there. Kee also let him know that if he kicked her door again, she was going to kick his ass. I guess Juan got the picture because he never came back to her door again.

After weeks of not going home, Kee and I decided to check on my apartment. When we walked in, it was a disaster. Juan had destroyed my apartment. He put holes in the wall with a hammer, tore all our pictures, broke dishes, and threw stuff everywhere. I was surprised we didn't hear him doing all that, especially since Kee and I lived directly across the hall from each other. Juan was so crazy that one day he set my headboard on fire while I was asleep. He was mad because I didn't want to have sex with him anymore.

Anyway, enough about him. Tay and Corey had finally arrived. I must say he was a nice-looking guy, and he definitely was my type. Corey stood about 6'5", medium built with braids. He was brown skinned with light brown eyes. If his eyes were one shade lighter, they would've been hazel. Tay introduced Corey to Kee and I, then he poured us a drink. We chilled, laughed, and got to know each other a little more.

Hours later, we had all passed out around the same time. Corey and I passed out on the love seat. Kee and Tay were passed out on the couch. The next morning, I was the first one to wake up. I grabbed my phone off the table to see what time it was. When I checked the time, I noticed I had ten missed calls and several text messages.

"Who's been blowing my phone up like this?" I said to myself.

At first, I thought it was Juan, but he hadn't called in over four months, thank God.

I glanced at the number and didn't recognize it. I

went to read my text messages and was shocked by what I read.

10:45 a.m.: Is Corey over there?

10:47 a.m.: This is Lele! Corey's girl. Tell him to get home now.

10:50 a.m.: Don't trust that nigga. He isn't shit.

10:55 a.m.: I swear I'm gone beat your ass when I find out who you are.

I laughed at the messages because one thing she didn't want to do was send threats. At that time, I wasn't wrapped too tight, and I didn't mind stomping her face in and removing her teeth from her gums. I didn't bother to reply to any of her texts because I didn't have time for the drama. Plus, Corey wasn't my man, and I wasn't trying to make him mine.

Minutes later, Corey woke up, and I gave him a crazy look.

"What's up, beautiful? Why are you looking at me like that?"

"This is why." I handed Corey my phone, showing him all the missed calls and text messages that Lele had sent me.

Corey shook his head then dropped it.

"I thought you didn't have a girl?"

"I don't. She's bitter as hell because I left her."

"How long y'all been broke up?"

"A week."

"A week! Really, Corey?" I said, giving him the side-eye.

"Look, I don't want her, and she's mad about that. I want to be with you, that's why I'm here."

"Hold on. Don't try to spit that weak ass game to me! For one, we only talked on the phone a couple of times, so there is no way you can possibly want me. You barely know me."

"I know a good woman when I see one. Don't act like when we had them conversations, you didn't feel what I felt."

I rolled my eyes. "Whatever.," I said, cutting the conversation short.

Kee and Tay finally woke up. I gave Kee that look, letting her know we needed to talk. Tay looked at the time and told Corey they had to go.

"Can I come back to see you tonight?" Corey asked.

"No! I'm good. I might be busy doing something more important."

Corey stared at me then laughed at my sarcastic remark. "Okay, I will hit you up later."

"Umm-hmm, okay."

"What's wrong with her?" I heard Tay ask Corey as they went out the door.

"Girl, why his girl been calling and texting my phone all morning?" I told Kee.

"What? Are you serious? Wait, I thought he didn't have no girl."

"I thought the same thing. Look at this shit." I handed Kee my phone to show her the text messages.

"Wow! That's crazy. So, what you going to do?"

"Girl, nothing. He's not my man."

"I saw the way that boy looked at you. I don't think he's going to let you go that easy. He stared at you the majority of the night," Kee stated.

"Oh, well."

Kee shrugged. "It is what it is, cousin. Girl, I'm not feeling Tay. He is not my type," Kee said, changing the subject.

I laughed. "Why? He's not ugly."

"Girl, did you see his arm? It looks like rubber."

We both burst out laughing. "What happened to it? It looked like he got burned."

"That shit looks nasty. I couldn't stop staring at it. I know one thing, after today, I don't think I'm talking to rubber arm no more."

"How you just going to name that man rubber arm?" I chuckled.

"Because that's his name." We laughed hysterically. The funny part is, Kee was so serious.

Corey wasn't even gone thirty minutes before he started texting my phone. He was apologizing for what had happened with his ex-girlfriend. I told him it was cool, and I wasn't tripping off that. For days, Corey begged to come over and spend time with me, but I kept giving him the runaround. Corey was persistent about coming to see me. I thought it was cute, but to be honest, I wasn't interested in him after his girl hit me up.

Although Corey told me they had broken up, in her eyes, they were still together. After days of begging, I finally decided to let Corey come back over Kee's house since I was still staying with her.

Chapter Fifteen

Days Later

"I apologize for what happened with my ex. I wanted to come over here and explain the situation between her and me."

"Talk," I said as I took a sip from my drink.

"I broke up with her about a week ago. We had been together for a couple of years. Things weren't working out between us, so I called it off. Every time I turned around, we were arguing or fighting over stupid stuff. I'm tired of it, to be honest. All a nigga wants is some peace. I'm not trying to rush you into anything, but I'm really feeling you. Just give me a chance to show you that I'm not who you think I am."

I sat there, not saying a word. For some reason, I

believed everything Corey said, but some men were good manipulators.

"You don't have anything to say?" Corey asked.

"No, not really."

Corey shook his head and smiled.

"What's funny?" I asked.

"You are. I love your little attitude. You're so cute."

I gave a fake smile, knowing damn well I wanted to smile from ear to ear.

"Look, just give me a chance. I promise I won't hurt you."

"I guess, but we're friends only."

After a couple of months, Corey and I became super close. We talked on the phone every day, all day. Even when we were at work, we made sure we were texting all day and calling each other on our breaks. Not a day went by that I didn't see Corey. He came to see me at least six days a week, and most of those days, he spent the night.

Lele played on my phone every day from morning to night. I don't know what Corey did to Lele, but she was going crazy over him. It got to the point that we both had to turn our phones off because she was blowing us up. It made her even madder when she realized I wasn't engaging in her pettiness. The crazy part is, I was the queen of petty. The only reason I didn't engage in her bull is that I was feeling Corey, and I didn't want to push him back to her. Corey had already told me that he argued and fought with her every day, so why would I want to cause more stress to the situation? Everything Lele was doing wrong, I made sure I did right.

I know this sounds crazy, but she made me want Corey even more. Now I was interested in what he had that was making her go so crazy. Months later, we finally made things official. Corey was very respectful, sweet, intelligent, and he had a genuine heart. What turned me on about him is he respected the fact that I didn't want to rush into a relationship or have sex. Not one time did he force me to be with him or to have sex. We just went with the flow.

Chapter Sixteen

Six Months Later

*L*ele was still playing on my phone every day, and I still wasn't replying. I got all types of text messages from her.

Stalker: *Bitch, I'm going to kill you when I see you.*

Stalker: *You better not fuck my man.*

Stalker: *Tell him I'm going to fuck him up.*

Stalker: *I'm going to kill both of y'all.*

Stalker: *You better not fuck him. He got something.*

Stalker: *I'm pregnant.*

Stalker: *He don't love you. He loves me.*

Stalker: *I swear it's over for both of y'all.*

Stalker: *I'm on my way to your house.*

Kee and I used to laugh at Lele so hard because she

was really in her feelings. I finally got tired of her playing on my phone and replied to her messages.

Look, bitch, I'm not even fucking him, but since you keep calling and texting, I'm about to. It's obvious he got something that you don't want me to have. Now I'm about to make his ass go crazy just like he is making you. Good day bitch!

Lele never replied to my message, and I was shocked. I guess she knew I meant every word I said. A couple of days after Lele texted me, I finally decided to have sex with Corey. I saw why she was going crazy. It was obvious the girl was dickmatized. She knew what he was working with, and she was afraid of someone else getting it. I wasn't the type to fall in love off sex; I always fell in love with the person. The sex was just a plus for me. I was more attracted to a man's brain than his sex.

Corey and I had been together for six months, and he was already in love with me without me spreading my legs. I loved him for who he was, not for what he had in his pants. We had a mental connection and a bond that no one could break, not even Lele. After I decided to have sex with Corey, he became possessive. He was already overprotective of me, but it got worse.

ONE DAY, COREY CALLED AND TOLD ME HE WAS ON HIS WAY over because he needed to talk to me. I told him that I would be waiting. I had no idea what he had to tell me, but I was kind of nervous. When he finally showed up to Kee's house, Corey asked if we could go somewhere private to talk. We walked into Kee's bedroom, and I shut the door behind us. I sat on the edge on the bed, and Corey stood in front of me.

"Look, Re, I don't know how to tell you this," Corey said as he placed both of my hands in his.

"Tell me what?"

Corey dropped his head, and I knew something was wrong.

"What? Tell me what's wrong."

"Lele is pregnant."

When he said that, my heart sank. It felt like my breath had left my body.

"Are your fucking serious, Corey?"

He nodded.

"Oh, we can't be together, then. It's over."

"You just going to throw everything we have away?"

"You threw it away when you cheated with her."

"I never cheated with her. She said she was pregnant before we broke up, but she never told me. I'm just finding out myself."

"How many months is she?"

"She claims she's five to six months."

I shook my head. "I knew I should've never trusted you with my heart."

"At least I'm being a man and telling you what happened, Re. When she told me, I made sure I came straight over here to you."

"Whatever. Just leave, Corey."

"What you want me to do? Not be a father to my child, because that's not happening. My father wasn't in my life, and I'll be damned if I don't be in my child's life."

"Okay, go be in your child's life, and leave me alone."

"I want you to stay with me. Just give me time to get everything situated, baby." Corey lifted my chin so I could look at him.

"Don't touch me. It's over, I don't want to be with you no more."

Corey begged and pleaded with me, but it was going in one ear and coming out the other.

"Please, just trust me."

"No. It's over, now get out."

Corey stared at me, then dropped his head.

"Re, just trust me, and hear me out."

"Bye."

Corey made his way out the door, and I burst into tears. I was so angry that I could've killed him. I told Kee what happened, and she couldn't believe it. Kee liked Corey, and she was rooting for us to make it. She used to always tell me that she loved the way he respected and treated me.

After crying my eyes out, I lay down because I had the worst migraine ever. On top of that, I had to get up at five o'clock in the morning for work. I didn't want to go, but I had no choice. My job didn't play about missing days or being late. I didn't fall asleep until around three in the morning.

I was so sick off what Corey told me that my mind was all over the place. Ne-Yo's first album played on repeat as I wallowed in self-pity. I played "So Sick" so much that I know Ne-Yo was tired of singing. My heart was broken. I knew that after this, I would never give love a chance, ever again. Soon as I got into a deep sleep, my alarm went off.

"Cuz, get up. It's time for us to go to work," Kee said as she tapped my shoulder.

My eyelids were so heavy that I could barely hold my eyes open. I went into the bathroom, washed my face, and got myself together. My eyes were red and puffy; it was clear that I had been crying all night. When we were done getting dressed, we made our way to the bus stop. I swear it felt like I was sleepwalking on the way. I couldn't wait to get on the bus and sit down.

THE ENTIRE DAY AT WORK, I COULDN'T FUNCTION. ALL I could think about was Corey. It was no secret how much I cared for him.

"Is it over between you and Corey?" Kee asked while we were on break.

"Yes, I'm done with him. He can be happy with her now."

"You know he doesn't want her, right?"

I rolled my eyes. "I can't tell. He got her pregnant."

"That was before you, cuz."

"So?"

"So, I think you should at least give him a chance."

"Fuck him."

Kee shook her head. "If that's how you feel, cuz, I can't do anything about it. At least look at the fact that he didn't cheat on you, and he was man enough to tell you."

I rolled my eyes again.

I didn't care about nothing Kee was saying at the time, even though she was right. My feelings were hurt, and all I could think about was myself. I can admit that I was stubborn, and the only thing I was concerned about at the time was my feelings. Corey's feelings weren't taken into consideration at all. I felt like Corey knew she was pregnant, and he held it back from me. I could've been wrong at the time, but in my mind, I was right.

I was jealous that Lele was going to have him for the rest of her life, no matter what. A baby was something I couldn't compete with. I felt like she had won everything, and I had lost it all, even though I knew deep inside that I had his heart.

❤

AFTER A LONG NINE HOURS AT WORK, IT WAS FINALLY TIME for us to get off. We clocked out then grabbed our phones out of the lockers. I had a hundred and twenty-five missed calls and seventy-five text messages from Corey.

"Cuz, did Corey call you?" Kee asked.

"Yeah, why?"

"Because I have over a hundred missed calls from him and twenty-five text messages."

I shook my head because Cory was losing his damn mind. I began to read the messages Corey sent me.

Corey Cell: *I miss you so much.*

Corey Cell: *Please talk to me.*

Corey Cell: *Can we please work this out? I never meant to hurt you.*

Corey Cell: *I know you at work. I just want to let you know I love you so much.*

Corey Cell: *I miss your pretty brown eyes and beautiful smile.*

Corey Cell: *Please talk to me.*

Corey Cell: *I can't live life without you, Re.*

Corey Cell: *Let me make it up to you.*

Corey Cell: I can't picture you with another man. I love you so much.

Corey Cell: Can we meet up when you get off work?

Corey Cell: It's now after 3pm. Why haven't you called me? I know you off work.

I shook my head because he was losing his damn mind. Those weren't even half the messages.

"Girl, please talk to him, so he can quit calling and texting me. Look, he's calling me now." Kee showed me her phone.

"I don't want to talk to him."

"Now he is texting, asking can y'all meet up."

"No. The way he is acting, he might kill me."

"I will be right there, cuz, just please talk to him. He deserves that much."

I rolled my eyes. "I will think about it."

Corey called my phone, and I declined his calls. He texted me and begged me to talk to him. I finally told him I would meet up with him, but it had to be in a public place. It wasn't that I didn't trust Corey, but the way he was acting had me paranoid.

After Kee and I got off the bus, we cashed our checks. When we were done, Corey texted me that he was waiting for me in the bar.

"I will be back. He's in the bar waiting for me."

"I'm right here if you need me, cuz. I'm not going anywhere. I'm about to roll up my joint and smoke," Kee told me.

Kee shook her head. "This is about to be a long weekend."

"To be honest, cuz, I just don't want to deal with no baby mama drama."

"If she wants drama, we can give it to her," Kee replied.

"In a way, I don't believe she's pregnant. I think she lied so she can get him back, but I'm not waiting around to find out."

"I do too, cuz. Just think about it. She had five to six months to tell Corey she was pregnant. Soon as she realized she lost him for good, all of a sudden, she's pregnant. That's bullshit, and she knows it. I'm not trying to tell you what to do, cuz, but I feel like he deserves another chance."

"I'm thinking about it, but what if it is true?"

"I doubt it's true. We will have to wait and see what happens. She's already five to six months, so we don't have long to wait."

"True."

Kee and I went home to get our weekend started. I took a hot shower and poured myself a drink. Soon as I sat down to chill, Corey called my phone. I wasn't going to answer, but I knew he would've kept calling or popped up.

"Hello."

"You busy?"

"No. Sitting here drinking."

"Why you didn't answer when I called the first time?"

"I didn't know you called. I was in the shower."

"Can I come talk to you?"

"What is it to talk about? We just talked for four hours."

"I want to talk about us. I didn't cheat on you. Can you get that through your head? We were just happily in love, and now you're saying fuck me. What I got to do to prove myself to you?"

"I don't know."

"You must have another dude. You back with your ex or something?"

"Maybe," I said, being sarcastic. I hadn't talked to or seen Juan in over nine months. Corey knew that, but since he wanted to be sarcastic, I could too.

"Don't fucking play with me. I will fuck both of y'all up, and that's on everything I love."

"Whatever." I hung up the phone, and Corey blew me up. I didn't even bother to answer him.

Corey: Why you keep playing with me? You going to make me turn into the devil himself. Call me back or we going to have big problems.

I read the text and continued to enjoy my night. I can't lie, I missed Corey and wanted to be back with him, but I just didn't want to deal with the baby mama drama if Lele was pregnant. My heart was telling me to take Corey back, but my mind was telling me that he was just like the other men.

An hour later, there was banging on the door. Kee came into the room and told me it was Corey.

"You want me to open the door?" she asked.

I shrugged. "I don't care."

"Where she at, Kee?" I heard him say as soon as he walked through the door.

"She's in the bedroom."

He burst into the room and slammed the door behind him.

"Why are you doing all that? It's not that serious, Corey."

"You think that shit funny?"

"What shit? I'm not laughing."

"So, you're messing with your ex now?"

"You know I'm not messing with him. You were being funny, so I decided to be funny with you."

"Re, look, all I want to do is make this right. Can we please do that?"

"Corey, I'm not trying to be dealing with her. I don't have time for the baby mama drama."

"You don't have to deal with her. I will make sure of it."

"You can't even control her from calling my phone every five minutes, so how the hell you going to make sure of it?"

"Trust me, I got this. So, are we going to work this out or not?"

"I guess, but I swear, if I have one problem with her, it's over between us."

A YEAR AND A HALF LATER

One day, Corey's boy gave us a ride to the liquor store and to KFC to get something to eat. Kee and I walked into KFC, and a dude who was selling CDs approached us.

"Hey, how y'all doing?" the dude asked.

"Fine," we said at the same time.

"What are y'all, Double Mint twins?" he joked.

Kee and I both chuckled at his remark.

"Would y'all like to buy some CDs?"

I heard a car door slam, and I looked out of the window, only to see Corey storming into KFC.

"What the fuck is so funny? Why you all in this nigga's face, laughing and shit?" Corey asked as soon as he burst through the door.

Everyone was staring at us while Corey acted an ass.

"He was just asking did we want to by some CDs, Corey," I replied.

"What's so funny about buying some CDs, Re? Nothing at all."

"You are tripping. Chill out," Kee told him.

My Mother Married My Rapist

"Nah, fuck that! Why you all in my girl's face?" Corey asked the dude who was selling CDs

"You know what? I'm not even hungry no more. You just spoiled my appetite. You are acting crazy for no reason." I stormed out the door then made my way back to Corey's friend's van.

"You all in that nigga's face like I'm not right here," Corey shouted as soon as he got in the van.

"You tripping. He was only asking us did we want to buy some CDs," Kee butted in.

"I don't give a fuck! Shouldn't no nigga be in my girl's face." Corey was screaming and going on and on.

I got to the point that I couldn't even argue with him anymore. Corey had quickly gone from zero to a thousand, and I couldn't wait to get out of the van and away from him. I wasn't an argumentative person, but once you push me to that level, it's hard for me to calm down. It took all of me not to argue with him. I was so mad to the point that I could've smacked his teeth out of his mouth.

We pulled up to our apartment complex five minutes later. I got out of the car without saying a word to Corey, and I didn't tell him bye or that I loved him. I was pissed to the max, and he knew it. Corey and I had been together for over a year. We'd never had an argument before. Soon as Kee and I walked into the house, Corey texted me.

Corey: *I will be back later, baby boo. Love you.*

151

Corey was texting me like nothing happened. I don't know if he'd forgotten the fact that he embarrassed us in public for no apparent reason.

Me: No, don't come back over here. I'm cool on you. You just showed your ass for no reason. When you come back, I won't be here. I got other plans.

Corey: What other plans you got?

Me: Plans that don't involve you. I will talk to you later when I'm available.

Corey: I'm on my way back!

Me: I'm gone already. Don't bother.

I knew exactly how to get under Corey's skin and piss him off. He didn't care about embarrassing us in public, so fuck his feelings. One thing about me, I hate when people put on a show in front of everybody. Stuff like that drives me crazy.

"Why you say that to that damn Aries? You know he isn't wrapped tight, cuz. You see how he just acted at KFC?" Kee said.

"I don't care about him being no Aries. He shouldn't have pissed this Pisces off. He should've thought about that before he embarrassed us."

"Let the war begin," Kee said, shaking her head.

I burst out laughing.

"I'm about to go hide down at Dee's house because I know he's on his way back. Don't tell him where I'm at."

Kee laughed. "You talked all that stuff, and now you're hiding."

I chuckled. "Shut up and let me know when he comes."

I made my way down to my friend Dee's house. Dee lived in the same building as we did, but she stayed downstairs. Dee had been living in the building for about a year or two. We were very cool and became the best of friends. She used to chill with Kee and I sometimes on the weekend. If I wasn't up at Kee's house, I was down at Dee's house chilling. I used to be at Nya's house, but she had moved out of the building a year ago.

Anyway, I went downstairs to Dee's house and told her I was hiding from Corey. She burst out laughing.

"What happened?" Dee asked.

I explained to her how Corey was acting crazy in KFC, but before I could even finish telling the story, my phone started ringing. I glanced down at it, and it was Corey. Soon as he stopped calling, Kee texted and said he was at her house.

Me: Is he gone yet?

Kee: No girl, he is searching my house from top to bottom. He keeps asking me where you at. I told him I don't know, but he doesn't believe me.

Me: He is acting crazy.

Kee: Very crazy. Girl, he just left and kicked your door in. I'm looking out my peephole. I hear him screaming your name talking about Sherri Marie Neal lol. He still searching your house. Thank God your door wasn't locked, or he would've torn the frame of your door off with that kick lol.

I burst out laughing.

Me: *He has really lost his mind.*

Kee: *You got that man going crazy. He is leaving your house now.*

Me: *Okay.*

I felt relieved once she said he was gone until I heard banging on Dee's door.

"Oh my God, that's him," I said to Dee as I hid on the side of the wall by her closet.

"Come in," Dee yelled from her bedroom.

"Why didn't you go to the door? Why would you let him come in?" I whispered. "Don't even look over here because he will know I'm in here."

Dee nodded.

"You seen Re?" Corey asked as he stood in Dee's bedroom door.

"No, I haven't seen her."

"You sure?"

Dee looked over at me then put her attention back on Corey. I just knew she gave me up when she did that.

"Yes, I'm sure," Dee replied.

"Okay, if you see her, tell her I'm looking for her."

"Okay, I will."

I was nervous as hell because all it would've taken was for him to step into her room and hit that corner.

Corey left, and Dee went to lock her door. Seconds later, I got a message from Corey.

Corey: *Re, stop fucking playing with me. You got ten minutes to show your face, or I'm going to start tearing shit up.*

I didn't know what he was talking about tearing up, and I wasn't trying to find out. I told Dee I would be back later and made my way to the back hallway.

Me: *I'm not playing.*

Corey: *Where you at? Show your face.*

Me: *I'm in the back hallway.*

I stood at the bottom of the stairs with my back against the wall. Seconds later, I heard Corey burst through the door. The door flew open so hard it put a hole in the wall. Corey stood at the top of the stairs staring down at me with rage in his eyes. The first thing I thought was, *he's about to kill me.* Corey took both of his black gloves off and threw them on the ground. When he ran down the stairs toward me with full force, I just knew he was about to put his hands on me. He threw a punch, leaving a hole in the wall beside my face.

"You lucky I love you because I want to break your pretty face. You so beautiful, I can't imagine putting my hands on you," he said as he pulled his fist out of the hole that he put in the wall. "Why you keep playing with me?" Corey placed both of his hands on the wall so I couldn't move.

155

"Because I don't like how you fronted on us in KFC, that's why."

"How you think I felt when I saw that nigga grinning all in your face?"

"Whatever, Corey. I told you what it was."

"Don't whatever me. Where were you when I was looking for you?"

"At my friend's house?"

"What friend's house? A nigga?"

"No, it was a girl," I said and rolled my eyes.

"Look, Re, I love you with all my heart, and I apologize for how I reacted. I'm just overprotective of what I love. Do you forgive me?"

I nodded. Corey gave me a hug then placed a kiss on my forehead. We talked in the hallway for a while until we had an understanding, then we went to Kee's house. For some reason, when Corey was mad at me, it turned me on. I guess I loved the attention and affection he would give me when he was upset. I knew Corey would never do anything to harm me, but I also knew that he would kill somebody if they tried to get close to me.

Corey was very overprotective of me, and that's what pulled me even closer to him. I wanted that protection; I wanted to feel secure at all times. I knew that he would never let anyone harm or hurt me. He cared about my feelings and everything I had been through in my life. Corey knew about my sexual abuse but not the whole story. He also knew about the abusive relationships that I had been in. A man couldn't even look at me the wrong way, or it would be a war.

Corey wasn't controlling, abusive, or manipulative toward me. He was just a man who was deeply in love, and he didn't know how to control his feelings.

Chapter Seventeen

A Month Later

*D*ee and I sat in her living room, talking and laughing. I can't remember exactly what we were laughing about, but it was funny as heck. The next thing I knew, there was a knock on the door. Dee opened the door without asking who it was, and I'll be damned if it wasn't Juan. It had been over a year and some months since I last saw him. Now, here he comes popping up unexpectedly.

'What are you doing here?" I said with my hands folded across my chest.

"I miss you, Mookie," he said, calling me by the nickname he gave me.

Juan tried to hug me, but I pushed him back.

"Get out of my face."

"I see you're not wearing the engagement ring I gave you."

"Can you leave, please?"

Soon as I said that, there was another knock at the door. I went to open the door, thinking it was Kee, and I'll be damned if it wasn't Corey. Corey looked at me then looked at Juan and back at me. I just knew that Corey was about to kill us both. Corey had never seen Juan before, but I guess he had a feeling that it was him.

"Oh shit," Dee said under her breath but loud enough for me to hear.

"Hey, I was just about to call you, Corey."

Corey's brown eyes had rage in them, and I knew he had a million and one things going through his mind.

"Who is that?" he asked with an attitude as he stared at me with anger in his eyes.

"That's my ex. He popped up out of nowhere."

Corey looked at Juan, and Juan was standing there with a grin on his face. That pissed Corey off.

"Nigga, what's funny?" Corey asked.

"Nigga, you."

"I will knock that Newport down your fat ass throat and make you choke on it, you fat motherfucker," Corey shouted.

"What up then, nigga. I will call all my people down here on your ass," Juan said as he reached for his phone.

"Nigga, what's up?"

Corey started walking toward Juan. I knew deep in

my heart that Corey would've killed Juan without a doubt. Juan was always a shit talker, but I had never seen him in action.

"Corey, please stop!" I pushed him into the hallway and shut Dee's door behind me.

Corey smacked my hand off his arm. "Don't touch me! What is he doing here?"

"He just popped up. I didn't know he was coming. I haven't seen or talked to him in a year."

"That's straight bullshit. I knew you was still messing with him. It's cool, though." Corey opened Dee's door. "You still in here talking shit? Nigga, what's up? I will beat the fuck out of you. Come in the hallway because I'm not going to disrespect Dee's house."

Juan stood there on the phone with his people, telling them what happened.

"Corey, just come on," I said as I pulled his jacket.

He left Dee's house and slammed the door behind him. "Re, don't touch me. Since he wants to call his people, I'm about to call mine. Trust me, I will be back," Corey said then went upstairs.

I knew things were about to get ugly. Juan had some crazy people in his family. Corey had a couple of boys from Chicago, and he was cool with a lot of hood niggas from Cincinnati. I tried to call Corey's phone and tell him not to do anything, but he wouldn't answer my call. I ran upstairs to Kee's house to tell her what was going on. That's when she said that Corey came upstairs to her house, mad as hell, and saying he was about to get his killers.

Kee told me that Corey asked her to promise him one thing, and she asked what's that. Corey told her to make sure she doesn't let anything happen to his keyboard then jumped out of her window. When Kee told me that, we laughed for weeks. I couldn't believe he jumped out a second-floor window and told her to watch his keyboard. That was the laugh of the year.

Chapter Eighteen

About an hour later, Corey came back with some of his people, and of course, Juan was nowhere to be found. They kept asking me where Juan was, like I knew. Corey and his boys sat up in Kee's house for a while, then they went outside to see if Juan was anywhere around. They waited outside for at least two hours. The entire time we were outside, I could feel the tension in the air between Corey and me. He kept staring at me with an evil expression. If looks could kill, I would be dead for sure.

Once they realized that Juan wasn't going to show up, Corey and his boys left. Corey swore up and down that I was being sneaky and talking to Juan behind his back. The way the situation happened, it did look like I was cheating. Although I wasn't doing nothing but standing there, I would've felt the same way if I walked in his boy's house and Corey's ex was in there.

For days, Corey and I argued over the situation. Corey wouldn't believe me for nothing in the world. The messed-up part is I was telling the truth about everything. I loved Corey so much, and I wouldn't do anything to jeopardize our relationship, especially not for Juan's cheating ass. One thing I can say about Corey is he didn't take me through half the stuff Juan took me through. I loved the fact that Corey had the utmost respect for me.

Juan was just a disrespectful bastard. He did everything in his power to hurt me. Lied, cheated, missed nights at home repeatedly, and put his hands on me. Juan was childish, and he didn't care about anything but sticking his shrimp dick in every girl's vagina.

After Corey calmed down, he finally came to talk to me. He apologized for not trusting me. He was just in his feelings when he saw me with another man.

I told him that I understood where he was coming from, and I apologized that it happened. Corey gave me a hug, and everything was back to normal. I knew that Corey still had doubts in his mind about Juan and me, though.

One night, Kee and I were coming home from somewhere. Kee spotted something black on top of the roof, and I'll be damned if it wasn't Corey watching us. He thought we didn't see him, but we saw him as clear as day. Corey used to always tell he had eyes on me, and I believed it.

♥

I finally moved from Ashwood apartments to a charming townhouse in a complex called Forest Ridge. The townhouse had three floors, three bedrooms, three bathrooms, and wall to wall carpet, plus a big balcony and a finished basement. After years of staying at Kee's house, I had finally moved into my new place. I was happy that Corey could finally come to my place. Soon as I moved in, I invited Corey over. We watched some movies and had a couple of drinks. Corey was there almost every night, and so was Kee.

One morning, I looked at my phone and saw that Lele had texted me. I was pissed off. The reason I was so angry is that I had gotten my number changed. The only possible way she could've gotten my number was out of Corey's phone.

"Good morning."

"Don't good morning me. How your ex-girlfriend get my number?"

"I don't know. She probably got it out of my phone."

"So, that means you been around her, right?"

"Yeah, but only to make sure my baby good."

"See, this is the bullshit I didn't want to deal with, Corey."

Corey dropped his head. "I can't win, can I?"

"Nope. You always getting busted."

"How? I never cheated or hurt you. So how I'm always getting busted?"

"Don't worry about it. Can you just leave?"

Corey grabbed his belongings and left.

Chapter Nineteen
ONE OF THE WORST DAYS OF MY LIFE

January 08, 2008

Kee and I were chilling at my dad and stepmother, Ava's house. We were laughing and having a good time. My phone rang, and it was my brother Don's wife.

"Hello."

"Sherri, your brother is in the hospital," Don's wife stated.

"What happened? Is he okay?"

"I don't know. Your nephew found him. I don't know if he's dead or alive."

"What! What hospital are you guys at?"

"Mercy hospital in Mt Airy."

"Okay, please keep me updated. I'm about to find a ride."

"Daddy, Brandy said Don is in the hospital, and she doesn't know if he'd dead or alive."

"Oh my God," Kee said and grabbed her chest.

"What! Hold on now. What you say?" my daddy said with a confused look on his face.

"Brandy said Don is in the hospital, and she doesn't know if he's dead or alive."

"He gon' be okay," my daddy said as he continued watching TV.

I immediately called my mother to tell her what Brandy had told me.

"Hello, stranger," my mother said as soon as she answered the phone.

"Ma, Don is in the hospital."

"For what?"

"I don't know, but Brandy said she doesn't know if he's dead or alive."

"What!" my mother shouted.

My line beeped, and I looked at my phone to see who was calling. It was Brandy.

"Hold on, Ma. This Brandy right here."

"God, please don't take my only son away from me," I heard my mother say right before I clicked over.

"Is he okay?" I asked as soon as I answered the phone.

"Sherri, he's dead." Brandy broke down crying on the phone.

At that moment, I felt all her pain. I was screaming

and crying uncontrollably. Kee was trying to comfort me.

"What the hell is wrong?" my daddy asked.

"Don is dead, Daddy."

"Say what? Oh, hell, nah." My daddy stood to his feet in disbelief.

I was screaming and crying so hard I woke my step-mama, Ava, up.

"What the hell going on in here?" Ma said as she ran into the room.

"Don is dead," my father told her.

The whole room was screaming and crying, including Kee. It was the worst news ever.

This was my only blood brother, and when I needed him, he was there. I didn't get to see him much because he worked like a slave, but I made sure I called him almost every day. A couple of months before he died, he had taken Kee and me somewhere. Before I got out of the car, he turned to me and said, "Sis, all you need to do is get a good job, find a good man, and get a car, then you will be straight."

"I know, right, but good men are hard to find."

"That's because you are searching in the wrong places."

I smiled and told my brother I loved him, then we went into the house.

The whole house was in an uproar. We were all affected by the bad news. I grabbed the phone to call my mother, and she began to cry. I didn't understand why this was happening. My brother was a good man. He was a hard worker, a husband, a father, a provider, and one of the realest you could ever meet. Me, Kee, and my dad rushed to the hospital as fast as we could. The question I had on my mind was, how did my brother die?

When we walked into the hospital, I gave Brandy a big hug. I can only imagine what she was going through. It had to be hard to lose someone you sleep next to every night. Brandy took us back to the room where my brother was, and he was lying in a bed with a sheet over his body. I almost fell to my knees, but Kee caught me. A pastor came along with some of Brandy's family members.

My father walked out because he couldn't take it. The pastor started praying, and I began to break down even more. I was sick to my stomach, and this felt unreal. I couldn't believe my only blood brother was lying there dead.

After the pastor was done praying, we walked out of the room.

"What happened to my brother?" I asked Brandy.

"When your nephew, Lil Don, got home from school, he found your brother foaming at the mouth, and his hands were reaching in the air. He ran and called 911. They said they tried working on him, but I guess it was too late." Brandy began to cry.

I hugged her and told her that everything would be alright.

We made our way toward the exit, so we could all leave. Soon as we got outside, a nurse came running behind us.

"Excuse me." We all turned around when we heard the nurse's voice.

"We forgot to give you this," the nurse said and handed Brandy my brother's wedding band.

Brandy opened her hand, and the nurse placed the ring in her palm. "I'm sorry," the nurse said then went back into the hospital.

That was the most heartbreaking shit I had ever seen someone go through. Kee's heart was broken when the nurse did that. My heart ached for my brother's son and his wife. My brother was all they had ever known. Don and Brandy had been together since their high school years. Now, the only man she ever loved had been taken away from her.

After we left, my daddy dropped us off at home in Ashwood Apartments. I called Corey to let him know my brother died, and he was shocked. He had just met my brother a couple of weeks ago. My brother joking with Corey and asking did he play basketball because of his height. Corey was 6'5" with a medium build. He was very respectful, for the most part.

My brother told Corey he needed to go play for the University of Cincinnati basketball team or the Lakers because he was too damn tall to be doing nothing. We laughed so hard at my brother. I cried for a whole week straight after my brother died. My heart was crushed, and I knew this would leave a hole in my heart forever. I cried so much before the funeral that I didn't shed one tear at the service except for when Kee sang, "His Eye Is on the Sparrow."

Oh, I forgot to tell y'all my girl Kee can blow. When I say she can sing, that girl can sang. Kee will blow the roof off the house or building, whichever one she is singing in. After the funeral, I grieved so hard. If it weren't for Kee, I probably wouldn't have gotten through it.

7-5-2008

My father came to stay with me for a while because he and my stepmother, Ava, had gotten into an altercation. Three days later, he told me he was going home to grab some paperwork, and he would be back soon. I told him, okay, and I would see him when he got back. A little while later, I received a phone call from my daddy, telling me to get over to his house because something was wrong with Ma. Me, Kee, Mia (Twin), and the dude Mia was talking to rushed over to my dad's apartment complex.

My dad and stepbrother, Deon, were standing

outside with a couple more people. The first person I went to was my stepbrother.

"Is Ma okay?"

Deon's hands were shaking fast, and he had tears in his eyes. "I don't know, sis," he replied.

"Daddy, is Ma okay?" I nervously asked.

"I don't know, Sherri," my daddy said with tears in his eyes.

Soon as he said that, the coroner rolled my stepmother out in a body bag. My heart stopped beating in my chest, and my mouth was wide open. I couldn't believe this was happening. I had just lost my brother five months ago, and now this. My heart was heavy, and I couldn't take it anymore. I looked over at my stepbrother, and he was crying and shaking. All I could do was wrap my arms around him and tell him it would be okay. This was devastating to me and everyone around. The pain was unbearable, and I was at a loss for words.

I can't even begin to explain the pain I felt. I walked over to my dad and gave him the most comforting hug. He had tears in his eyes, and I could feel his body trembling as I hugged him. I glanced over at Kee, and she was crying. Hell, everyone there was crying. We sat around for a while, then we finally left. When we got home, my dad told me what happened, and this was what he said.

"Before I left a couple of days ago, I left the key under the pot on our balcony. When I got there, I looked under the pot for my key, and it was still there. I thought to myself that Ava must not have been home since I left, and that wasn't like her. I walked through the living room to get to my bedroom then went into the closet in my bedroom to grab my papers. When I turned around, I noticed a big hump under the cover. I thought that it was maybe some folded clothes under the covers from how high it was sitting.

"I walked closer to the bed, and that's when I noticed a person lying there. I yelled, 'Lady, who are you? And what are you doing in my bed? But I didn't get a response. I pulled the cover back, only to see that it was Ava. The only reason I recognized her is because of her nightgown. Ava had dried up blood and foam all over her face. It looked like she had a mask on. Ava's body had blown up so big, I could tell she had been there for days. I called the police and waited outside for them to come."

All Kee and I could do was cry our eyes out. Five months ago, my nephew found my brother dead, and now my daddy had just found my stepmama dead. The only mother I could depend on, the only mother who believed I was sexually abused, and the only mother who would cuss me out one day and love me the next. The only mother who would whoop anybody's ass over me, the only mother who taught me how to cook, the only mother who took me in as her own, the only mother who loved me unconditionally. No, not my Ma. This couldn't be life. This couldn't be true.

My father blamed himself for a long time. He felt that if he had just gone home, maybe he could've saved her. Come to find out, my stepmother died from a heart attack, the same thing my brother died from. Ma had a funeral, but she didn't have a burial because she got cremated. Damn, this shit hurts to write. I wonder how life would be if I still had my loved ones.

—RIP Ma—You will always be my mother, no matter what.

RIGHT AFTER MA PASSED, I GOT A PHONE CALL WHILE I WAS in college that one of my favorite aunts had passed away on my daddy's side. Man, my aunt was the sweetest woman on this earth. She always had a smile on her face, no matter what. I couldn't believe this shit. Like, our family was getting hit back to back with death.

At one point, I began to think that our family was cursed. Soon as my heart tried to start the healing process, somebody else would die. Damn, I love you, Auntie. May you rest in peace —Rip Auntie Lulu

Chapter Twenty

Corey and I had been dating for four years. Our relationship was good, but we still had our problems. One thing I can say is we had more good times than bad. Besides the incident with Juan, we didn't have any issues. We had good communication skills, and we made sure we showed each other the utmost respect. In four years, I hadn't had one problem with another woman besides his ex-girlfriend Lele.

As time went on, things began to take a turn for the worse. After my brother died, I began to shut down. That messed me up mentally for a while. After my brother passed, Kee stayed with me for a while. She helped me out with the kids because I became depressed. I started feeling like I was going to die because my brother died. Corey would come and stay with me when he wasn't working. I eventually started to get better. Although I was depressed, I didn't show it when Corey came around. I knew he felt it, though, because he would always ask what was wrong, but I would say nothing.

FAST FORWARD

After four long years, Lele had started back playing on my phone. I knew she had to have some type of mental issue to still be doing that. One night after making love to Corey, I got a text from Lele.

Stalker: *Bitch, I'm going to kill you and him. I know where you live because we been following him.*

Me: *If you think you big and bad, come on, bitch! I will be waiting.*

"Why she keeps texting my phone, Corey? I'm sick of this."

"I told you she bitter, Re."

"You need to put that bitch in check. She already lied about being pregnant."

"I can't control what she does. She a grown ass woman."

"If you think I'm about to deal with this stupid bitch any longer, you got me messed up. I will be in jail for murder, and that's on my life."

"So, what are you saying?"

"I'm saying control her, or it's over."

Corey and I got into a big argument, and I told him it

was over between us. I told him to leave and lose my number. This time, I had my heart made up. Lele continued to text my phone that night. I ignored her until she said she was on the way. One thing I didn't take lightly was threats. Somebody was going to die that night, and it wasn't going to be me or anyone in my household. I didn't play about where my kids laid their heads. Lele was about to get the ass whooping of her life, and she didn't even know it.

Kee and I both grabbed a knife and put it in our back pocket. We had a bat by the door, pepper spray, and hot water boiling on the stove. We even had a cup of bleach waiting by the door with Lele's name written on it.

Stalker: *Bitch, I'm outside. Come out.*

I didn't bother to text back. I went straight to the door to open it. Surprisingly, she wasn't outside. I could tell that she had been there, though, from the fresh footprints that were in the snow on my porch. God spared her life that night; it was going to be murder she wrote.

THAT SAME NIGHT, I GOT A MESSAGE FROM LELE SAYING she was pregnant again. Here we go, going through the same shit again. I called Corey to see if it was true.

"Is he pregnant, Corey?"

"She claims she is."

"So, that means you slept with her, right?"

"It just happened, Re. I didn't mean it. It was only one time."

"Look, I love you, Corey, but I can't do this no more. I'm tired of her playing on my phone, sending threats, and I'm tired of you lying to me about her."

"I'm sorry, baby."

"It's over," I said then hung up.

How dare he have sex with this girl after all she took us through when we first met? I couldn't even find the words to explain how hurt I was at the time. My heart was broken into tiny pieces.

Corey texted and called my phone for weeks. He asked for closure, but I didn't give it to him. I was so angry with him that I never answered his calls or texts, and that was the end of us. I had been with Corey for four long years, and he was one of the best men I ever had. I didn't have to deal with the bull that I dealt with from other men in my past. Corey showed me how I was supposed to be treated. He was the one who made me realize I was worth more than what I was settling for.

Corey helped me get my self-esteem back intact. Not a day went by that he didn't tell me I was beautiful. I knew Corey loved me to death, and I knew it affected him tremendously when I left. He should've thought about that before he cheated on me.

. . .

THE NEXT MONTH

I sat on the toilet, staring at the pregnancy test that read positive. I couldn't believe I was pregnant with Corey's baby. Part of me wanted to keep it, but the other part of me didn't. Instead of calling Corey and letting him know I was pregnant, I took it upon myself and had an abortion behind his back. I felt so bad afterward, and that shit ate at my conscience for a long time. If Corey ever found out I had an abortion, I knew he would kill me without a doubt.

I regret having the abortion because I did it out of anger. I was young, dumb, and stubborn. All I cared about was my feelings at the time and no one else's. Corey was still in love with me. Instead of working things out and giving each other closure, I left. I was trying to find myself and figure out this thing called love.

As time went on, I found out that Lele wasn't pregnant. She lied because she knew that was the only way to keep Corey around. Lele even admitted that she knew I had his heart, and she was jealous of me. When I found that out, we had already been broken up for months. I felt dumb for letting her come between what we had, but it still didn't change the fact that he cheated with her. That shit hurt because I trusted him with my heart, and for that reason, I wasn't ever going back. Plus, I had already moved on with my life. Although I still loved Corey, I didn't want him back, especially after I heard he went back to Lele's retarded ass. I wasn't about to deal with that headache all over again.

Corey was miserable without me for years from what I heard. He and Lele were still fighting every day all day. Corey told someone that he regrets letting me go, and that was one of the biggest mistakes he's ever made in his life. Corey said to someone that I was the best woman he ever had, and the next man would be a fool not to keep me. If he had one more chance, he wouldn't mess it up.

I never saw or heard from Corey again. I prayed to God to send me the right man for my kids and me, and I promised myself that I was going to be single until God sent me the right one.

Chapter Twenty-One

2009

*M*y friend, Nya, had been going through health problems over the years. She was a heavyset girl, and the doctors told her she needed to lose weight. The weight was affecting her health tremendously. Although Nya had health problems, that didn't stop her from living life. One thing I can say about Nya is she might've been big, but her confidence was even bigger. She was the true definition of big and beautiful. Nya was comfortable in her skin, no matter what. She was so pretty, and her smile could light up a room.

I used to always tell her she reminded me of the comedian Monique. She was funny, cute, and she kept it real whether you liked it or not. Nya had the biggest heart, and she was always there for everyone. She loved her family to death. Nya's daughter, mom, big sister, and nephews were her heart.

One day, Nya told me she had to get a pacemaker. I was so scared for her; all I could do was pray. I could tell Nya was frightened, but she kept a good spirit about the situation.

Nya finally got the surgery done, and I was happy when she told me everything had gone well. I made sure I checked up on her every chance I got. Months after that, Nya told me that the doctors had given her five years to live. *Her exact words to me were, forget what them doctors say. It's up to God, not them.* Nya was still smiling and in good spirits. I remember that day like it was yesterday.

ONE DAY, I WAS SITTING AT HOME CHILLING WHEN I GOT A phone call saying that Nya was in the hospital. I called Kee and told her we had to get to the hospital as soon as possible. After I picked up a couple more people we knew, we were on our way. When we walked in, I wasn't expecting to see Nya in the condition she was in; she was on life support. Tubes were down her nose and throat. Everyone in the room was in tears.

No matter how hard we tried to be strong, we just

couldn't do it. We tried to talk to Nya, but she couldn't respond. A couple of times, it looked like she was trying to say something, but she couldn't get it out. It broke my heart to see my friend like that, and if I could've taken the pain away, I would've.

Nya was pronounced dead at the hospital on my sister's birthday, June 18, 2009. This when I started questioning myself about life. What was the purpose of living if we were going to die anyway? What if I died next? Who would raise my kids? Why did people close to me keep dying? Is life worth living? Why did good people die? All those questions were in my head.

I had become so afraid of death that I was scared to fall asleep. I thought that I wouldn't wake up the next day. Everyone close to me seemed to have been taken away. I lost my brother, my stepmother, my aunt, and now Nya. This couldn't be life. Losing so many people close to me was a hard pill to swallow. I wished that it was all a dream, but unfortunately, it wasn't. I had to wake up and face reality.

Every night, tears covered my pillow as I thought about my loved ones. I tried to remember all the good times when it came to Nya, but I kept picturing her suffering in that hospital bed. Watching her mother lose her baby was hard to do. I prayed to God to let me leave this world before my kids. The pain that Nya's mom went through was heart-wrenching.

After Nya's funeral, it still felt unreal. I was still

calling her phone, wishing she would answer. If I could see Nya one more time, I would tell her how much of an impact she had on my life. Nya taught me to love the skin I'm in and keep it real no matter what.

R.I.P., I love you always.

Chapter Twenty-Two

My sister had been battling breast cancer for the last couple of years. Tia and I (Twin) made sure we visited my sister a couple of times a year in Atlanta. The cancer was eating my sister up bad, but we knew she would beat it. Chelly went through the stage of losing her hair, and that made her feel down, but she learned to cope with it. After that, she had to get one of her breasts removed. (Her right one if I'm not mistaken.)

My sister was very depressed when she got her breast removed. Chelly would call me, crying and saying she looked like a monster. I used to tell her that she didn't, and she was beautiful just the way she was. My sister cried her eyes out on the phone with me.

One day she called and told me that she was cancer-free. I could hear the happiness in her voice. Chelly said she was going to celebrate with Chuck her fiancé.

♥

ONE DAY, MY SISTER CALLED ME. SHE SAID SHE NEEDED TO ask me a question. This was before she had cancer.

"What's up, sis?"

"Did Patrick really do them things to you?" my sister asked.

"Yes! Why you asked me that?"

"Well, because Ravine (my oldest niece) told Mama that Patrick grabbed her breast. When Mama asked Patrick about it, Patrick said that they were playing, and it was an accident.

"Don't believe that. That's the same thing he used to say when he did it to me. Trust me, if he did it once, he will do it again."

I told my sister everything Patrick did to me and didn't leave out anything. Although she knew some of it, she didn't know the whole story.

"Mama told me that you were lying on Patrick because he wouldn't give you what you wanted. I didn't believe it, though."

"Bonnie a lie, and the truth isn't in her. Mama believes anything that man says."

My sister told me she believed me because she had revealed some secrets about Patrick herself. She said she saw an email on Patrick's laptop that read, *did you tell your wife you were burning yet?*

"Wow! No need to tell Bonnie because she isn't going to believe it, Chelly."

"I know."

My sister and I continued to talk for a while, then we hung up. I don't know if my sister ever told Bonnie, and honestly, I don't care.

I RECEIVED A PHONE CALL FROM BONNIE SAYING THAT MY sister's cancer had come back, and it was more aggressive than before. This time, it was lymphoma. It started under her armpit and rapidly spread. The doctor in Atlanta couldn't do anything for her, so my sister decided to go to the Oklahoma cancer center to see if they could help her.

When she got there, they ran tests on her, and she felt like she had hope. I made sure I called my sister every day to check on her. If I didn't call her, she called me. A couple of weeks after my sister got to the cancer center, she caught pneumonia. The pneumonia was attacking my sister's lungs bad. The doctor told Chelly they may have to put her on life support if it got worse. Let Bonnie tell it, my sister told the doctors she didn't want to be on life support, living like a vegetable, and to let whatever happens happen.

The pneumonia began to get worse day by day. When I would talk to my sister on the phone, she could barely breathe. For every word she said, she had to pause to take a breather. One day, my sister called me.

"Sherri, I have a question."

"What's up, sis?"

"The kids are in Atlanta with Patrick, and I don't really trust it. Do you think they are safe there with him?"

"Hell no! I'm telling you, sis, Patrick is a nasty, perverted ass child molester and rapist."

"I believe it. I'm about to call Aunt Janice and ask her to go get them. I will call you right back."

My aunt Gee lived in Starkville, Mississippi, which was about four to five hours away. She was our aunt on my mama's side. Aunt Gee was my mother's only sister, and I loved her to death. After my sister got off the phone with our auntie, she called me back.

"What she say?" I asked as soon as I picked up the phone.

"She said she will go get them for me."

"Good."

"I just don't trust Patrick like that, especially since mama told me he grabbed Ravine's titties a while ago. To be honest, I never trusted him or cared for him."

"I don't blame you, sis. I'm glad somebody is starting to see how he is."

We talked a little while longer then we disconnected our call.

6/27/2009

I was over a friend's house, having a drink. My phone rang, and it was my mother.

"Hello."

"Hey."

"Hey, Ma, what's up?"

My mother took a deep breath. "Your sister died."

"What! Are you serious?"

"Yeah, she's gone."

I began to cry, and I couldn't even talk on the phone anymore. I felt like God was punishing me; I just couldn't get a break from this shit. My brother, my step-mama, my aunt, Nya, and now my sister, all gone in less than a year. This shit was taking a toll on me. I grew up with a brother and sister, now it was only me left. I had nobody to talk to or cry to when times got hard. I mean, I had Kee, my dad, and Dee, but it was nothing like that sibling love. I would say my heart was broken, but that would be an understatement. My heart was damaged, destroyed, and numb.

The pain I felt on that day is unexplainable. I was on the floor crying and sick to my stomach. How could God let this happen? I questioned. My sister was such a good person, and she had a good heart. Although

Bonnie tried to destroy our relationship with lies, we still were close. My sister got to know me for herself and saw that I wasn't the girl that Bonnie and Patrick were making me out to be. We had our ups and downs, but what sisters didn't?

My sister and I were closer than people thought. I could talk to my sister about anything, and she would always give me good advice. When she had problems, especially men problems, she called me. Even though I was younger than Chelly, my mentality was older, so I would give her good advice when needed.

When Chelly was sick, she told me how most of her friends in Cincinnati turned their backs on her. She would reach out to them, but she would never get an answer. Chelly felt some type of way about that, but I told her I had her and not to worry about anything. I couldn't do much because I was in Cincinnati, but I made sure I called her and went to Atlanta to check on her.

Tia and I went at least five times a year, if not more. Many people thought that my relationship with my sister wasn't good. What they didn't know is that over the years, we became super close. When she got sick, we became even closer. I was happy that my sister got to know me for who I really was years before she died because we had some the best times of our lives. Whether it was on the phone or when we saw each other, it was always love.

. . .

ATLANTA, GA

7/4/2009

I got out of the car and prepared myself to say my last goodbyes to my sister. Although I wasn't ready, I had no choice. I hugged my nieces and nephew, then me, Twin, and my daddy made our way to my sister's casket. I stood there, staring at my sister, and hoping that she would wake up and say she was ready to go home. Chelly looked so peaceful; I'm almost sure she made into heaven.

After we finished saying our goodbyes, we took a seat. I looked over at my father, and he was wiping tears from his eyes. I had never seen my father cry the way he cried that day. My father was a strong man, so to see him drop a tear hurt like hell. It was finally time for them to close the casket, and that's when my sister's boyfriend, Chuck, lost it.

"Please don't leave me, Chelly," he said as he cried over her casket. "I love you so much. Please don't take her away from me." Chuck was hugging my sister and kissing all over her.

That made me and everyone else break down. I could see the hurt and pain in Chuck's eyes, and I felt so bad for him. I wish I could've taken the pain away, especially from my sister's three children. They were so hurt that their mama had left them.

Hours after the funeral, Bonnie got a call saying that Chuck was lying next to my sister's grave, drinking, and he wouldn't leave.

"I don't know why he's doing all that hooting and hollering. He didn't love my daughter," Bonnie said with a nasty attitude.

"What makes you think he didn't love her, ma?" I asked.

"Because if he did, he wouldn't have been cheating on her."

"That don't mean he doesn't love her. He just made a mistake. We are all human."

The nerve of Bonnie to say that Chuck didn't love my sister. I knew he loved her. No matter what Chuck and my sister went through, he made sure his family was good. My sister loved Chuck to death, and I knew that for a fact. What I didn't understand was how my mother was judging Chuck when her man liked little innocent girls. I guess that didn't matter, though.

Anyway, Chuck tried to get custody of the kids, but my mother got custody instead. Months after my mother got custody, they moved to Starksville, Mississippi. I felt bad that Chuck's kids were taken away from him because they were all he had left. I felt even worse when I found out that Bonnie and Patrick's perverted ass would be raising them. I knew it was only a matter of time before Patrick started molesting my nieces and nephew.

. . .

Y*EARS LATER*

It had finally come out that Patrick was molesting my older niece, Ravine. I called Bonnie to confront her about the situation.

"Hey, Mama. What's going on with Ravine?" I asked, getting right to the point.

"Ravine claims Patrick been molesting her. I think she only saying that because of what happened to you."

"Ma, Ravine never knew what happened to me unless you told her."

"I didn't tell her nothing. Maybe somebody else did, but I didn't. Let me call you back," Bonnie said with an attitude.

Bonnie never called me back, so I made it my business to call her, but she wouldn't answer any of my calls. I called my Aunt Gee, and she informed me that my mother didn't want to talk to me because she was mad. That was typical ass Bonnie for you, always mad at the wrong people for the wrong reasons. When was she going to get it in her head that her husband was a rapist and child molester? That was the person my mother should've been mad at.

I called my niece, Ravine, who was sixteen years old at the time and asked what Patrick did to her. The stuff she told me was the same thing he used to do to me. My niece exposed some things to me that Patrick did, and that shit blew my mind. It made me sick to my stomach, and my adrenaline was rushing. I knew he was sick in the head, but this was beyond sick. How could a grown man be so perverted and hurt an innocent child? I wanted to shoot Patrick and watch him die slowly after what Ravine told me. How dare he do that shit to my niece after all she had been through.

I asked Ravine how long Patrick had been molesting her, and she told me since she was seven years old. She went on to explain how things got worse after her mother died. I was hurt that I was all the way in Cincinnati, and I couldn't do anything about it.

The first thing I said to my niece when she was done talking is, "I believe you if nobody else does." I told my niece that I would call her back.

I googled Starkville, Mississippi police station and called their number. When they answered, I explained what was going on with my niece. The person who answered connected me to the detective. I told him that my niece was being molested, and the detective wasted no time handling the situation. The detective brought Ravine in for an interview, and days later, they arrested Patrick.

He wasn't even in jail a good forty-eight hours before my mother bailed him out. The detective arrested him again on another charge, and Bonnie bailed him out again. He got locked up at least three times, and each time, Bonnie broke her neck to get him out. Bonnie took

Chapter Twenty-Three
MEETING THE LOVE OF MY LIFE

August 2009

*I*t had been almost two and a half years since I had been in a relationship. I had promised myself that I would only focus on my kids and me until God said otherwise. I had finally gotten a car, a house on Section 8, and I was a toddler teacher at a daycare. Life was going great for me, and I was in a happy place. Even though I was a single mother, that didn't stop me from grinding for my kids. It was a struggle raising three kids on my own, but I did it.

I didn't have help from either of my children's fathers. Davonna's dad had finally started paying child support when she turned seven years old, and that helped me a little. I still struggled, but I kept things afloat. Long as my kids had shoes on their feet, clothes on their backs, a roof over their heads, and food on the table, we were good. A lot of people used to ask me how I took care of three kids at the age of eighteen, and my reply was always God. Without God's grace and mercy, I couldn't have done it.

August 2009

"Every time I see that dude, Blu, I can't get him off my mind," I said to Dee as we lay across her bed watching TV.

Blu was a dude I had seen a few times in my old neighborhood.

"Oh lord, here you go."

"I'm so serious. I don't know what it is about him."

Dee shook her head and laughed.

"I'm about to go to his house."

"It's late," Dee said as she glanced at the time on her cell phone.

"I don't care. Are you coming or what?"

"You know I am."

We slipped on our shoes then made our way down to Northside, where Blu lived. I was nervous because I had never approached a man before; they were always approaching me. Although I wasn't sure if he'd noticed me, I damn sure noticed him. Word on the street was he had a girl, but he was on the verge of leaving her. That made me kind of skeptical about getting to know him because I didn't want to deal with the drama, especially after what I went through with Corey's ex.

Dee and I pulled up in front of Blu's spot. We knocked on the door, but we didn't get an answer.

"Maybe it isn't meant for me to get to know him," I told Dee as we walked back to my car.

"Ahy." We heard a dude's voice say from across the street.

We looked over and saw Dee's boyfriend, Johnathan, and a group of dudes.

The first thing I peeped was Blu's brown Dickie coat that he used to wear. "Oh, my God. Girl, there he goes," I said with a big Kool-Aid smile and butterflies in my stomach.

Dee burst out laughing.

We hopped in the car and drove to the parking lot across the street. I didn't know how I was going to approach Blu because, like I said before, I had never approached a man a day in my life. We pulled up, and Johnathan walked over to the car.

"What y'all got going on?" Johnathan asked.

"Nothing," Dee and I said at the same time, sounding sneaky.

"Aww shit, what y'all on? Y'all look like y'all on some sneaky stuff."

"We not on nothing," I replied. "Sike, nah, tell your boy, Blu, I said what's up."

"You tell him. Ahy, Blu, she wants you."

I hit Johnathan on his arm. "Dang, you didn't have to say it out loud."

Blu glanced at me then walked over to the car. All his boys were staring, trying to see what I wanted with Blu. I went to my text screen on my phone and wrote *I want to get to know you* then showed it to him.

Blu smiled and told me to lock his number in my phone. It was something about him, but I couldn't put my finger on it.

Chapter Twenty-Four

The Next Day

"Y ou got a girl?" I asked Blu as we sat on the steps in an apartment building at Ashwood Apartments.

"You want me to tell you the truth?"

"Of course, I do."

"I won't really call her my girl because I been trying to get rid of her for the longest."

"Why is that?"

"Because it seems like she doesn't want shit out of life. All she does is sit around and leach off me all day. Don't get me wrong, I don't mind taking care of my woman, but she's not bringing nothing to the table. This girl has stolen from me, cheated, and tried to have sex with my cousin. I been trying to get rid of her ass, but she won't leave," Blu said as he took a pull from his joint.

"What you going to do?"

"I don't know."

After hearing Blu's problems, I told him that we should take things slow and keep it on a friendship level. I didn't want to get in the middle of what he had going on in his relationship. Plus, I wasn't playing second best to any woman.

Over time, Blu and I became the best of friends. We talked to each other every day, all day. Blu would come over my house to chill and watch movies with me. Sometimes he would ask for advice about his relationship, and I would give him some good feedback. Everything I told him to do to fix his relationship didn't work. As time went on, I could feel the bond between Blu and I growing stronger. Every morning, Blu would text me, *Good morning, beautiful. I pray you have a blessed day,* and every night he would tell me not to forget to pray before I went to sleep. That turned me on to him even more, but I kept it on a friendship level.

Months after we started talking, we both started to express how we felt.

"I want to be with you, Re."

"How? You got a girl."

"I told you, I don't want to be with her."

"Well, why you with her?"

"I'm not with her. She won't leave."

"Seems like you got a problem on your hands. When you get rid of her, we can discuss us."

"Okay, smart ass."

I chuckled.

Bad as I wanted to tell Blu yeah, I just couldn't. I refused to jump into a relationship with a man who had baggage. I had been there, done that, and refused to do it again. I would be single for the rest of my life before I dealt with another man's problems with women, especially after what I went through in my last relationship. I needed to know for sure that he was done with her before I made any decisions.

Actions speak louder than words, and I was all about action. One day, I was lying across my bed, thinking about Blu. Soon as I was about to text him, he texted me.

Blu: I want to be with you. I know you feel the same.

Me: What makes you think that?

Blu: I can feel it.

Me: Look, I want to be with you too, but I'm scared. I been hurt too many times, and I refuse to get hurt again.

Blu: You can't control love, Re. You know that, right? I'm going to give you two weeks to think about it then I want my answer.

Me: Lol. Whatever.

I couldn't believe Blu had given me a deadline to be with him. I thought it was cute. Although I wanted him just as bad as he wanted me, I had my guard up. I understood what Omarion meant when he said, "I got an icebox where my heart used to be."

I wanted to commit to Blu, but I was afraid of being hurt. I started to think about all the pain and heartbreak I went through in my past relationships. The more I thought about it, the more I didn't want to be with Blu or anyone else for that matter. I didn't know if he would eventually hurt me or leave me for his ex. Was he genuine about everything he was feeding my mind and soul? It felt real, but that didn't mean it was. I had a brick wall built up around my heart that nobody could break down. I knew that one day I would eventually have to take a chance at love; I just didn't know when that day would come.

Yes, I wanted Blu badly, but I wasn't expecting a relationship this soon. I wanted to get to know him and become friends with benefits. I wasn't expecting for feelings to get involved so fast. I wasn't expecting our connection to be so strong after months of knowing each other.

Two weeks later

"Did you think about it?" Blu asked as soon as I answered the phone.

"I'm still thinking about it."

"Don't think too hard."

"I'm not."

Blu and I talked for a couple more minutes, then we disconnected our call.

I couldn't believe this man remembered to call me for his answer. To be honest, I thought he was just talking, but he was serious about us being together. Later that night, I finally gave Blu his answer. When I told him yeah, he was super excited. We became intimate days later. When I say he has the best sex I ever had. I would tell you about it, but I might have to kill you. The way he explored and got to know my body turned me on. Every time we made love, I could feel the chemistry and love between us. We couldn't get enough of each other.

Blu and I were together every day. If we weren't together, we would be on the phone all day from the time the sun rose until it set. Sometimes we would fall asleep on the phone with each other. I knew in my heart that he was my soulmate; I could feel it. It felt like we had known each other for years, and it had only been a couple of months. We had an unexplainable connection, and I had never felt that connection with any other man.

When I was thinking about him, he would call me as if he felt me thinking of him. I would be thinking something, but before I could say it, he would say it. Sometimes we would say the same thing at the same time. We could feel each other's emotions without saying a word.

If we were on the phone, and I was upset, he would feel my vibe. I knew this man loved me deeply, but I still questioned myself about him. It was nothing he did; I was just afraid of heartache.

Blu paid attention to me and noticed things that no man had ever noticed before. He knew when I was mad, happy, or sad without me saying a word. When I had something on my mind, he knew it without me telling him. Blu almost knew me better than I knew myself, and that was scary. I've never had a man to observe me the way that Marcus did; that's Blu real name. He gave me all types of chills and goosebumps over my body when I was around him. I've never had this feeling from any man. This was a different kind of love.

The bond he shared with my kids was incredible. Blu loved my children like they were his own. My kids loved him also and respected him like he was their father. I respected Blu to the fullest for accepting my kids and being a father figure to them. I used to thank Blu all the time for being such a great stepfather.

Blu hated the word the stepfather. He would always say, "I'm not a stepfather. I'm the father who stepped up, and you don't have to thank me because that's what a man is supposed to do." That made me love him even more.

What really put the icing on the cake is this man prayed with me. I had never met a man who was willing to pray with me. Most of the men I dealt with didn't even mention prayer, or God, for that matter. Whenever I was feeling down, Blu would pray with me or tell me to pray. Not only did he pray for me, but he also prayed for my kids.

Chapter Twenty-Five

Weeks after Blu and I made it official, I began to have problems with his ex. I told Blu to handle it, and he did exactly that. After we were together for about four or five months, Blu was sentenced to some time in jail for violating his probation. I was hurt and lost for words when he told me he had to do some time. I wanted to smack the shit out of him. The man I was madly in love with was going away. My feelings were hurt, and I didn't know how I was going to cope without him in my life. I couldn't feel his touch and make love to him when I wanted to.

This was tearing me apart, and I didn't know what to do. I guess I couldn't be mad at anyone but myself. That's the type of stuff you have to deal with when you are dating a dopeboy. Marcus asked me to wait for him, and I told him I would. Weeks later, he turned himself in to Hamilton County Justice Center. While Blu was in jail, we talked at least three to five times a day. We wrote each other at least twice a week, if not more. I made sure I kept his spirits up while he was in jail. Every time we talked, he asked about the kids and how they were doing in school.

Blu also made sure I wasn't stressing over him being away. When I had bad days, Blu would lift my spirit. He always knew the right words to say to make me feel better. When I visited him, the whole time, he would smile at me and tell me how much he loved me. I could tell that my presence made Blu's day.

Blu had been in jail for a month when his ex decided to start playing on my phone with her friends. I guess she thought I didn't know it was her. What she didn't realize was that I was the queen of petty. I made sure I made her life miserable in every way possible. Once I got into my petty mode, it was hard for me to stop. One thing about me, I was an investigator. I could find out your phone number, family members' name, social security, birthday, every job you worked. Hell, I could even find out a person's blood type if I needed to. My friend, Dee, used to always call me a private investigator.

As time went on, I finally left her miserable ass alone. I only did it because I didn't want Blu to find out that I was feeding into her childish bullshit. Although I told him what his ex did, I never told him what I did to her in return until later in the relationship. After a while, I started to feel like Blu was still messing with his ex, but let him tell it, he wasn't. I believed him to a certain extent, but my woman's intuition got the best of me.

Come to find out, my feelings were valid. One day, while leaving visitation, the receptionist gave me all the pictures his ex had sent him. I didn't know why she did it, but I felt like she did it on purpose. I asked Marcus did he ask her to send him pictures, and he said no. After that, I started to question his loyalty and began to question myself. Was this the man for me? Is he really messing with his ex? Does he still love her? Is he going to get out and go home to her? Is this jail talk? Those were some of the questions I asked myself daily. I also prayed to God that if this was the man for me to keep me with him. If not, remove him from my life.

"I can't believe they gave you her pictures. They did that shit on purpose," Kee said as she took a pull from her joint.

"I know they did. What if he still loves her, cousin?"

"Girl, please. That man loves you without a doubt."

"What if he leaves me for her?"

"Trust me, he isn't going nowhere, Sherri. That boy loves you."

"What if he does?"

"If if was a fifth, I would be drunk as hell. Stop with

the what ifs, cousin. That man loves you to death. The way he looks at you and admires you. The way his face lights up when he sees you. The way he prays for you, girl, you can't tell me that man doesn't love you. You and the kids are all he thinks about."

I rolled my eyes. "I'm scared, cuz."

"I know, but you got to learn to trust and love again, cousin." Kee shook her head. "You know what, you a make a bitch smoke a whole quarter in a day. Matter of fact, let me roll up again because it's about to be a long day. My brother doesn't want that girl," Kee said, referring to Blu. "The only reason he was with her is that she takes cucumbers in the booty."

We both burst out laughing. "Where the hell that come from?" I asked, barely able to breathe because I was laughing so hard.

"I mean, look at her. She's not even cute, for real, and I'm not saying that because you're my cousin. She big as hell, and her ass sits on her shoulders. I hope she doesn't consider that a big ass because it's not. It's just wide as hell."

I chuckled. When Kee got high, she started letting people have it, and she didn't give no fucks who you were.

"Look at you. You're beautiful, you got a lot going for yourself, you dress cute, you keep yourself up, and you want something out of life. All she wanted to do was take cucumbers in her ass."

I laughed. "Cuz, I can't stand you."

"I'm just saying, that boy loves you. He tells me all the time. Cuz, don't let your heart stop you from having something good."

After Kee was done talking to me, she prayed for me and Blu's relationship.

Chapter Twenty-Seven

After doing eleven months in jail, Blu was finally released. Me and Tia (Twin) picked him up, and we went straight to my house. Kee had a fat joint rolled up and waiting for him as soon as he walked into the house. I couldn't believe I had my man back in my arms. Our bond and chemistry were stronger than ever before.

"I told you I was coming home to you, didn't I? Quit doubting me, Re. My word is my bond, baby. I keep telling you that."

I playfully rolled my eyes because every time I thought this man was going to let me down, he proved me wrong.

"I told you I want to be with you. Why don't you believe me? You need to let that wall down that you built up and start trusting in your man more," Blu said then kissed me on the cheek.

"Umm-hmm, you probably just saying that," I sarcastically said.

Blu dropped his head. "You just don't get it, do you? What I feel for you is real. This shit isn't a game."

"Prove it."

"I'm trying to, but you keep putting your guard up. I'm not them other niggas who hurt you, so stop blaming me for what they did to you," Blu said then walked away.

I was speechless because Blu was right. I was punishing him for the hurt and heartache of my past. The sexual abuse, physical abuse, cheating, lies, low self-esteem, and betrayal had me afraid to give him my all. The crazy part is, Blu didn't even know my past, but he could tell that I had been hurt and mistreated. This was exactly why I loved this man. Blu knew that I was damaged on the inside, but he still took a chance on loving me.

As time went on, I told Blu about my sexual abuse, physical abuse, and mistreatment by men. That drew him even closer to me and made him overprotective. Blu told me that no matter what I had been through, he loved me regardless, and we were going to get through this together.

I told Kee this man is too good to be true. Girl, pinch me because I had to be dreaming. Kee used to laugh at me so hard. Her response was always, *"that boy loves you to death. I can feel it in the air. I love him like a brother for loving you. You deserve to be happy, cuz. Let that man love you and stop giving him a hard time."*

Kee would always pray for our relationship. She wanted us to make it, and she made that clear to me all the time. I loved Blu, but as you can see, I had some issues with giving him all of me. I was holding back because I was afraid of being hurt. I felt like he would switch up on me like everybody else.

Chapter Twenty-Eight

Blu started talking to me about moving in about three months after he got out of jail. It felt like he was already moved in if you asked me. He was at my house every day, and the majority of the days, he stayed overnight. Blu had his own apartment, but he let his cousin rent it out while he stayed at his mom's house.

About a month later, Blu called and told me he was moving in with me soon. I thought he was lying until one day he showed up with some of his belongings. It wasn't all his stuff, just a couple of bags.

"I told you I was moving in. I'm not completely moved in with you yet, but I will be soon," Blu said as he placed his bags in the closet. "I love you, Re," he told me.

I was speechless. Here I was doubting him, and he

proved me wrong again. I prayed that when he moved all the way in, it wouldn't mess up our relationship.

Blu's mother had started calling him every five minutes. I didn't know why, and I didn't bother to ask. I could tell that whatever she said was pissing him off. I noticed he started going to his mom's house more often than usual, and I began to question it.

"Why you always at your mama's house now?" I asked.

"Because she's my mama, that's why. It's not like I live here yet."

"Don't play me like I'm stupid, Marcus, because I'm not. I see how mad and frustrated you be when you have to go up there. Your ex still lives there, don't she?"

"No, boo."

"Marcus, stop lying to me."

"It's complicated. I promise I will talk to you about it when the time is right."

"The time is right now."

"It's not. Trust me, please."

I rolled my eyes and didn't say anything else about it.

Gradually, I began to shut down from trusting Blu, because, in the back of my mind, I believed that he was still with his ex. I started questioning if this was the man I really wanted. My mind was telling me not to trust him, but my heart was saying something different. I began to go back into the shell that I was once hiding in.

The bricks that were around my heart began to build back up. It felt like I was going through the same thing I went through in my past relationships.

On my birthday (Feb 28th), Blu took me to a restaurant called Tumbleweed on Colerain Avenue. That's when he explained why he had been at his mama's house.

"Look, I'm about to keep it all the way one hundred with you. My ex has been staying at my mother's house. I have told her plenty of times to leave, but she won't. I thought when I came to stay with you for a while, she would get the picture and leave. Instead, she stayed there. My mother kept calling me and saying that my ex wasn't her responsibility, and I need to come back over there. I began to get frustrated with the situation.

"My mama called me for days, but I didn't bother to answer. She sent me text messages saying I need to come back and tell her to leave. I went back to tell her, but she wouldn't leave, no matter how many times I told her it wasn't working out. I'm here to tell you that you are all I want. I don't want that girl. I been fell out of love with her before I met you. I'm not going to lie, I have love for her, but I'm not in love with her. The woman I'm in love with is you."

My heart told me that this man was telling the truth, but my mind was questioning it. You ever had somebody tell you something, and you believe it, but you still have that little doubt in the back of your mind? It felt like an angel was on my right shoulder, telling me to believe him, and the devil was on my left shoulder, telling me he was lying. It was playing tug of war with my heart. I didn't know what to believe, but I was always told to follow my heart.

"You sure about that?" I asked.

"I'm positive."

"How I know you won't go back to her?"

"Because I won't. I keep telling you my word is my bond."

"Did you get her out of your mother's house?"

"No, but she claims she's leaving."

"Okay, we will see."

"We sure will. Now, let's enjoy the rest of our night. It's your day, baby."

We enjoyed the rest of our dinner, and afterward, we went to the casino to finish the night.

Chapter Twenty-Nine

lu's mom, Ms. Robin, and I began to have words. She was mad about something Blu's ex told her.

"I don't know why y'all arguing over Marcus. He doesn't love y'all. That's lust," Blu's mother, Ms. Robin, stated when I answered my phone.

"Who arguing with her? Not me. I just blew my horn at them since they kept hitting the brakes while I was driving behind her and her friend."

"Well, like I said, Marcus don't love y'all. That's lust. Y'all fighting over a man who don't do shit for y'all but give y'all a wet ass!" Ms. Robin shouted.

"I don't know what he does for his ex, but he takes care of me. As a matter of fact, he just got my car fixed and took me out to eat."

"I don't know where he got the money from because

I take care of him and Tanya," she said, referring to his ex.

"Don't be telling her my damn business," Tanya shouted in the background.

"Who the fuck you talking to?" Ms. Robin asked her with an attitude.

"You!" Tanya shouted back.

I sat on the phone while they argued like two childish teenagers. On the inside, I was laughing hard as hell.

"Girl, you aren't talking to me anyway. Well, since he does all that for you, ReRe, did he tell you his ex went out of town with us last week? Did he tell you that?" Ms. Robin asked.

"No, he didn't."

"Exactly, because he doesn't care about you or her. Like I said, lust."

"He must care because he moved some of his stuff in my house to be with me and not her." I knew that would piss them both off when I said that.

"Oh, he did? Well, tell him he can come get the rest of his bullshit out my house. Tell Marcus that," Ms. Robin said with an attitude.

"I sure will," I said then disconnected the call.

I questioned Blu about going out of town with his ex, and of course, he denied it. We argued for at least two hours over the phone and texts. I knew deep in my heart that Blu was lying to me, so I told him it was over and to bring my car. I wasn't about to accept disloyalty at all. I stayed at my friend Dee's house that night. Around three in the morning, Blu started blowing my phone up.

"What?" I said with a nasty attitude.

"Can we talk?"

"No. I'm cool on you. Talk to that bitch. Park my car outside and leave the keys under the seat."

"You didn't even give me a chance to explain."

"It's nothing to explain. Did she go out of town with you and your family?"

"I'm outside. Come get in the car so we can go home and talk."

"Don't ignore me. Answer the question."

"Man, just come outside, so I can talk to you, Re."

"No, I'm cool on you."

Blu started blowing the horn like he was crazy.

"Can you stop blowing the horn? People are sleep. You going to get her put out."

"I'm going to keep blowing it until my woman come talk to me."

"Here, I come." I blew my breath then disconnected the call.

The entire way to my house, I rode in silence. Blu was talking, but I wasn't. I needed time to calm down before I responded, or it was going to get ugly. Minutes later, we pulled up to my house.

"Re, the shit don't look as bad as you're making it," Blu said as soon as we walked into my bedroom.

"How would you feel if I took my ex out of town?"

"Man, look, I didn't take her out of town. I didn't want her to come. That was my mama's doing. I should've told you."

"You damn right, you should've told me. You got me out here looking stupid as hell."

"You never looking stupid. If anything, she's the one looking stupid. Everybody knows that I'm in love with you."

"Whatever."

"Can we work this out? I promise it won't happen again."

"How do I know that?"

"Because my word is bond, and I will do whatever to prove that shit to you. That's on my soul, baby."

"I don't even feel right being with you after I got into with your mama. I don't want to be beefing with the man I love's mama."

"Man, I will jeopardize my family for you, baby. I won't go around them until you feel comfortable, and that's on my life. My mama pissed me off doing that bullshit anyway. I don't understand why my mama did that when she knows I don't want to be with that girl. You have to excuse my mama, though. She's petty like that."

I shook my head. "I guess we can work it out, but from here on out, no more secrets."

"Okay, baby. Will you go with me to get the rest of my belongings from my mama's house in the morning?"

"Yeah, I will."

When I told Blu that his mother said to come get the rest of his shit, that was all he needed to hear. That was his key to get out while he had a chance.

The next morning, Blu woke me up so we could go get the rest of his belongings. We pulled up to his mother's house about fifteen minutes later. While Blu was in his mother's house, I called my friend, Dee, and told her to come outside. Dee and Mrs. Robin stayed across from each other. We stood outside talking while Blu loaded his belongings into the car.

"They salty he's leaving. Look at his mama in the window," Dee said, and we both burst out laughing.

"Oh well, she shouldn't call my phone on that bull."

"I feel you, girl. That boy loves you. I can tell."

"You think so?"

"Yes, I really do."

Dee and I talked until Blu was finished loading the car, and then we left. Blu didn't go around his mother, and he barely spoke to her on the phone. I felt like it was all my fault, and that made me feel bad. Blu explained to me that it wasn't my fault. He told me that his mother was always keeping some unnecessary drama going, and this wasn't the first time. Blu explained to me how his mother was negative at times, and he was tired of it.

As time went on, I finally got to see it with my own eyes.

For about six months, Marcus kept his distance from his mom. Once again, I doubted him. I thought he was lying about Jeopardizing his family, not like I wanted him to. When I told him that I was ready to be around them, he gradually started bringing his mother around. Blu made sure that I was all the way comfortable first. Sometimes his mother would say slick stuff to me, but before I could respond, Marcus would put her in her place. Marcus made it clear to his mother that he loved me. It was either she respected me or don't come around at all.

Over time, his mother and I grew to love each other.

Chapter Thirty

As time went on, Marcus and I fell deeply in love. We had the type of love that other people wished and prayed for. Nothing or no one could come between what he had. Plenty of people tried, but it didn't work. People started to become jealous of our relationship. We began to lose friends and family, but we stood strong together. People used to think that we were this perfect couple, and we didn't have problems. I would be lying if I said we didn't. We had more problems than a math book; we just didn't let other people solve our problems. Any problem we had was worked out in the privacy of our home.

Don't get me wrong, we went to our friends and family sometimes, but we learned our lesson from that. We started keeping our relationship and household business to ourselves. When you keep people out of your love life, your relationship runs smoother. You don't have to deal with people being judgmental or the negative remarks. Life is so peaceful without the extra opinion that's not needed.

In 2012, I discovered that I was pregnant with Marcus' first child. That was one of the happiest days of our lives. I was delighted that I could give Marcus his first child. The day I told him I was pregnant, he was happy, but in denial at the same time. At the time, I had only taken a home pregnancy test. Marcus told me to go to the doctor because he needed to see it on paper. I went to the doctor the following week and brought Marcus back the paper, and he still was in denial.

"I'm so happy, baby. I can't believe that I'm about to be a father. You don't know how long I prayed for this. I finally get to experience my woman carrying my baby."

"I'm happy too."

Marc got off the couch and gave me a big hug. During my pregnancy, he made sure that he was at every appointment. I remember he acted a fool at my first appointment because the doctor stuck his fingers inside me to examine me. I had to tell him to calm down and that it was part of his job.

I was sick the first four months of my pregnancy; I couldn't keep anything down. It seemed like as soon as I found out I was pregnant, the sickness began.

On January 3, 2013, I gave birth to a beautiful baby girl. We named her Promise Lee'chell Fairbanks. We named her Promise because we promised to always love and respect each other, no matter what. We got her middle name from Marc's great grandma (Perrie Lee), who raised him, and Chell from my sister, Chelly, who passed away. Marcus' great grandmother made a big impact on his life, but unfortunately, she passed away months before we met. I wish I could've met her because he always spoke very highly of her. His grandmother definitely raised a good man.

About a year after Promise was born, Marc, the kids and I joined a church called Lincoln Heights Baptist Church. We went a couple times before we joined. Marcus was more familiar with the church than I was because some of his family were members there. Although we joined the church, we weren't going as often as we should. Most of the time, we would pray and have church in our home. Marcus always told me that as long as you keep the faith and know God in your heart, you're good.

Chapter Thirty-One

Although things had been going well between Marcus and me, I still sometimes questioned if he really loved me. He just seemed too good to be true. It had been five years, and I was still questioning his love for me. I was so used to getting my heart broken that I thought eventually he would hurt or leave me.

"Baby, do you really love me?" I asked Marcus.

"Of course. You know I love you, boo. Why are you still questioning my love for you? Haven't I shown and done everything you asked me to do?"

"Yes, you have."

"So, why are you still questioning it?"

"Because I'm scared you will leave me or cheat on me like the rest of these men did."

"Don't compare me to no other man because I'm me. All this do you love me, and cheating questions every day is starting to drive me crazy. I've been with you for five years, and you still ask me the same questions. What else do I have to do to prove my love to you, Re? I give you reassurance whenever you need it, I tell you I love you every day, I tell you how beautiful you are, I take care of you and my kids, I'm home every night to you, I answer all your calls, I make love to you daily, I cook when you want me to, I clean, and I pray with you. What else do you want me to do?"

"Nothing. I appreciate everything you do for me."

"Why you keep questioning my love for you then? What is it going to take for you to let that wall down that you got over your heart, Re? Soon as you let it down, you put it right back up. Don't part-time my love. I need that shit full time. I don't part-time your love; I make sure I love you full time."

"I'm sorry. I just be so scared, baby."

"You don't have to be scared. I'm here to love you, not hurt you. We're going to always have ups and downs, but I'm here for eternity. I'm not going nowhere."

I hated questioning Marcus about his love for me. I knew he loved me, but it was too good to be true. I was so used to being hurt, mistreated, abused, and taken advantage of by men that I thought he would do the same. I told Marcus how much I was hurting from being sexually abused. At times, I would have flashbacks when we were having sex. I would start crying or continually tell him to stop.

One day, he was sucking on my right breast. I moved his head and told him to stop because it made me think about when I got molested. Marcus said that made him not want to touch me anymore, and it made him feel uncomfortable. He explained that he didn't want to trigger any of my sexual abuse, and he wasn't going to touch me again. Marcus also said that he wanted to shoot Patrick's ugly ass for what he did to me. He felt like he should be able to enjoy his woman without her feeling uncomfortable, but he understood that it wasn't my fault.

I felt bad because I shouldn't have to stop my man from doing what he wanted to me because of my past. That shit hurt like hell.

WHILE IN CHURCH ONE SUNDAY, A PASTOR FROM OUT OF town was preaching. He was speaking about forgiveness. He said, "If someone hurts you, you need to forgive them and let God handle the rest. When you hold hate in your heart, it's not good for your spirit. You got to let go and let God. You are giving that person control of your life when you hold grudges and don't forgive. If that husband cheated on you, forgive him. If that friend was disloyal to you, forgive. You can't keep holding on to stuff that happened ten, twenty, or thirty years ago. You must forgive. If that mother hurt you, forgive. If that brother hurt you, forgive. If that man shot you, forgive. If that man raped or molested you, you have to forgive. God's vengeance is way better than ours, and trust me, they will reap what they sow," Pastor shouted from the pulpit.

When the pastor said that, something came over me. Have you ever been in church and felt like that message was for you? I felt like Jesus was telling me to forgive Patrick for what he had done to me. I had already forgiven my mother, but I never forgave Patrick. I told Marcus that Jesus wanted me to forgive Patrick. Marcus said that whatever I decided to do, he was with me. He also told me to listen to God.

I kept saying to myself, *I'm not forgiving that perverted bastard. Forget him.* I mean, he molested and rape me, but I didn't do anything wrong to him. I even told Jesus he was tripping, and he lost his damn mind. Yes, I cursed at Jesus, and trust me, I paid for it. God made me eat those words quicker than I said them. Jesus put it so heavy on my heart for weeks to forgive Patrick, and I didn't have a choice but to call.

I hesitated with the phone in my hand for at least thirty minutes. I prayed then I finally made the call.

"Hello."

"Hey, Ma. What you doing?"

"Hey, nothing. Sitting here, watching TV. How are

you doing, Ms. Lady?"

"I'm fine. Where Patrick at?'

"Right here."

"Oh, can you tell him that I forgive him for what he did to me?" I rolled my eyes.

"I will let you tell him. Hold on."

I tried to take the easy way out by having my mother tell him, but it backfired on me. I guess Jesus was like, *Nah, you aren't getting out of it that easy.*

"Hello." The sound of his voice made me want to throw my phone out the window. I hated his voice! Hell, I hated him period.

"Hi, Patrick." I rolled my eyes. "Jesus give me strength, please," I said to myself.

"Hey, Sherri. How are you doing?"

"Fine."

"That's good to hear."

"I was calling to tell you that I forgive for what you did to me."

"Aww, thank you, Sherri. I really appreciate that, and I'm sorry for what I did to you." The shit didn't sound sincere at all when he said it, but I guess. "I love you, Sherri."

"Okay, put my mama back on the phone."

I knew he didn't think I was about to say I love you back. It was kind of creepy that he would tell me he loved me anyway. I wondered what my mother was thinking when he said, *I'm sorry for what I did to you.*

Patrick had basically admitted his crimes, but of course, she was too blind to the shit.

My mother got back on the phone, and I could hear the happiness in her voice. I guess she thought things were going to be different because I forgave Patrick. I might've forgiven him, but I will never forget. I will never be in the same room with that man a day in my life if I could help it.

I talked to my mother for a couple more minutes, then we hung up. I felt much better after I forgave Patrick. The hurt I once had in my heart toward him began to fade away. It didn't go away overnight, but it did eventually. My sex life got way better, and I started to feel more comfortable. I still had flashbacks from time to time, and that's normal. Like I said before, I can forgive, but I will never forget.

I thought about going to counseling or therapy for it, but I felt it would be a waste of my time. I felt like I could get over it on my own. Marcus told me that before I went to counseling to let God be my counselor. I took his advice and started talking more to God about my sexual abuse. The more I prayed, the more I started to feel relieved from my abuse. My mind and heart started to become at ease.

Chapter Thirty-Two
THE WORST HEARTBREAK EVER!

January 24th, 2017

anging on my door woke me up. *Who banging on the door like they the police?* I said to myself. I opened my door, only to see my big cousin, Rodney, and my Aunt Carla standing there.

"Hey, Auntie, come in," I said as I wiped the sleep out of my eyes.

"Sherri, I got something to tell you."

"What are y'all doing here? Is everything okay, Auntie?"

"Dan is dead."

Tears began to stream down my face. My heart stopped beating in my chest, and I could barely breathe. I ran into my bedroom, where Marcus was sleeping and began to scream.

"Boo, Daddy is dead."

"What!" he said and jumped up.

Marcus saw the tears running down my face, then pulled me into his arms and held me tight.

"I'm so sorry, baby," he said as tears ran down his face.

I got the strength to walk into the living room to talk to my auntie. I asked her what happened, but at the time, she wasn't sure. She just told me he died in his sleep. We talked for a while, then she told me they were about to head back to my daddy's house. After they left, I broke down to my knees. Marcus was in the bathroom throwing up because he couldn't stomach what I had just told him. Marcus and my father had a tight bond. My father loved him like he was his own son.

After Marcus finished vomiting, he got dressed so he could go over to my father's house. He kept saying he didn't believe it, and he had to see it with his own eyes. Marcus asked did I want to go, but I couldn't see my father like that. I couldn't believe my father was gone. It felt so unreal because I had just talked to my dad the night before. I could still hear the conversation in my mind.

"Hey, Daddy, what you doing?"

"Oh, nothing, about to head to Kroger to get me some fruit then to my sister's (Aunt Carla) house. What y'all doing over there?"

"*Nothing, Daddy. I was just calling to check on you and make sure you're okay.*"

"*Oh, okay.*"

"*Okay, Daddy. I love you.*"

My daddy hung up so fast that he didn't hear me say it. Usually, I would call back, but that particular day I didn't. I felt terrible when I learned he was dead the next day. I blamed myself for a long time for not calling him back that day. Marcus told me to stop blaming myself because my father knew I loved him.

I called my family and friends to let them know what happened, and they were devastated. The first person to make it to me was Kee. She was crying and hugging me tightly. I could tell she didn't want to let me go. Kee knew how much of a daddy's girl I was. When Tia got off work, she also came over to spend time with me and a couple of my other friends. My kids took it very hard when they heard the news. That was the only grandparent they knew on my side of the family. They knew Bonnie too, but not like they knew my dad.

A couple of days later, I had to go to the funeral home to plan my father's funeral. That was the hardest thing I ever had to do. I wasn't ready to say my farewells yet. This wasn't supposed to happen like this. I thought my dad would at least live long enough to see his great grandkids. This was the most devastating situation I ever had to face in my life. I couldn't believe my father was really gone. This was the time I wished my brother and sister were alive, so we could hold each other up.

It was unbelievable to me that my sister, my brother, and my father were gone. I came into the world with two siblings, and now I was the only one left. This was a hard pill to swallow, and it was very hard to cope with.

Once I pulled myself together, I called my aunt to find out what happened to my father. Supposedly, he had a heart attack in his sleep. In my heart, I believed his girlfriend, Laura, killed him. When she found him dead, she didn't even call 911. Instead, she called my auntie. Not to mention, she had my father's suit in the cleaners already, his shoes shined, and Laura tried to get my father's house switched over in her name the same day he passed away. She had all my father's belongings by the door to give to Goodwill, but I told her she better not touch anything.

I didn't trust that lady one bit, and I never did. Even when my father was alive, I would say she was weird. I called the detective, and he said he didn't have a reason to question her, although she wasn't showing any emotions when he watched the body cam. I called the coroner to see if they had the autopsy report for my dad, but they said they didn't have my father's body there. I called my aunt Carla, and that's when I learned that Laura had sent my father's body to Walker's Funeral Home.

I told my aunt that Laura didn't have permission to

send my father's body anywhere. My aunt Carla told me that Laura told the police that she was his wife, and that gave her permission to get his body sent to the funeral home. One of my cousins told me to find out if my father had been embalmed yet, so I could get an autopsy done. I wasted no time calling, but I was too late. The man told me he had just finished embalming my father.

I wanted to kill Laura's ass because I knew deep in my heart that she took my father away from me and his grandkids. If I ever find out, it's going to be hell to pay for her. Another thing that didn't sit right in my spirit was that my father's insurance policies were changed to accidental death except for one. I knew that all my father's insurance papers weren't for accidental death. Months before he died, he updated all his insurance policies. He brought me copies, and they all were whole life insurance policies. None of it made any sense.

Laura also slipped and told my aunt that she was happy about my father's death. When my aunt checked her about what she said, Laura tried to switch up and say she only said it because he was suffering. That wasn't true at all. Yes, my father was sick. Yes, my father did have heart surgery, but he was okay. My father had gone to the doctor seven days before he died.

When I called to tell his nurse he passed away, her exact words were, "Oh my God, what happened?" When I told her that he died from cardiac arrest, she said, "I can't believe it. That's so hard to believe. I just saw your father last week, and he was doing great. He had no complaints, and he was functioning fine. Everything looked great. I'm so sorry. He was such a good guy."

That right there gave me every reason to believe that Laura had killed my father. Not to mention, she wore all red to the funeral. I heard when you wear all red, it means you're happy that the person is dead.

At the funeral, Laura told my oldest daughter, Day-Day, that she was very jealous of her and my father's relationship. Thank God, my daughter told me after we got home because I would've whooped her ass for saying that to my child.

Almost a week and a half after my father passed away, we had his funeral. My father was a sergeant in the Vietnam war. When we pulled up to the cemetery, the honor guard was waiting. They draped my father's pure white casket and carried it to his burial site. The firing squad fired three volleys and played Taps. Next, the guard did the ceremonial folding of the flag. When he was done, he presented it to me in honor of my father.

Oh, how I miss my old man. If I could have one last time with my daddy, I would lay in his arms and tell him how much I love him. I would hold my father so tight and never let him go. I love him so much, and my heart still aches to this day. Not a day goes by that I don't think about him. I kiss his picture almost every day. I wished heaven had a phone because we would be talking right now.

My father was so funny; he kept us laughing. I used to always tell him he acted like Pops off the movie *Friday*. I miss him so much, and I didn't know how I was going to do this thing called life without him. Whenever Marcus and I needed him, he was always there, no matter what the situation was.

I miss you, Daddy, and may your soul rest forever.

Chapter Thirty-Three
THE HAPPIEST DAY OF MY LIFE!

March 03, 2017

I sat inside BJ's restaurant, enjoying my birthday dinner with family and friends. It made me so excited to see everyone there, especially after losing my dad a month and a half ago. I was overly glad that Marcus put this birthday dinner together for me.

As I conversed with my friends, Marcus told me he was about to go to the restroom. I told him okay and kept running my mouth like always. Minutes later, someone called my name, interrupting my conversation. I turned around, only to see all four of my kids and Marcus standing there with red shirts on. Each child had a word on their shirt. Promise's shirt said *Boo*, Makayla's shirt said *Will*, Davonna's shirt said *You*, Quanterrious' shirt said *Marry*, and Marcus' shirt said *Me?* I couldn't believe my eyes. My heart was racing, and I had butterflies in my stomach.

Marcus handed me a dozen roses and got down on one knee.

"I love you, baby. Will you marry me?"

"Yes!" I excitedly said.

The whole restaurant cheered along with our family and friends. Marcus stood to his feet, and I did the same. I gave him the biggest kiss and hug ever. I would've given him more, but people were around. Haha. I was so excited that I didn't want to let him go. I couldn't believe Marcus had proposed to me; it was like a dream come true. I thought this day would never come.

We took some pictures with family and friends. Afterward, Marcus took me to the Embassy Suites hotel. He had rose petals from the door to the bedroom and all over the bed. Candles were lit everywhere. The whole night, we talked, laughed, and made love.

Months later, we had an engagement party. Our family and friends showed up and showed out. That was one of the best nights of my life. A night I will never forget.

Once again, I had doubted Marcus. I thought he would never marry me, but he showed me differently like always.

Chapter Thirty-Four

"Ma, I'm moving to Atlanta with Grandma," my daughter, Davonna, said as she stood in my kitchen.

"No, you're not. I don't trust Patrick."

"Ma, people change. Patrick might've changed. You never know."

"He hasn't changed. He just molested Ravine five years ago. I know for sure that man hasn't changed."

"You never know, Ma."

"Day-Day, I don't want you to go, but you're old enough to make your own choices. Just be careful because he's a pervert."

"I really don't think he's like that no more, Ma, but okay, I will be safe. I wish he would touch me. I will kill him," Davonna said with a serious look on her face.

"Why you want to move down there anyway?"

"Because I want to better myself, Mama. I know if I move down there, I will have a better chance of being successful and fulfilling my dreams."

"I understand, Day-Day."

Deep down inside, I didn't want Davonna to leave because I was worried about what would happen to her. Davonna didn't know my mother and Patrick like I knew them. No matter how much I tried to convince Davonna, she had her mind made up.

A month later, Davonna moved down to Atlanta with my mother and the pervert.

Four days after Davonna moved in with my mother, she called me.

"Ma?"

"Yes, child."

"I got something to tell you, but you got to promise me you will stay calm."

When she said that, I already knew it was about to be something bad.

"What happened, Day-Day?"

"Patrick kissed me while I was sleeping. At first, I thought I was tripping. When I finally got my eyes to adjust to the light, nobody was right there. I looked over to my left and saw Patrick standing there, acting like he was looking for something. When he left the living room, I got up to see what he was looking for, and nothing was there."

"I told you that nasty, perverted bitch didn't change. You need to leave now before I come kill his ass."

"Ma, I got this. Trust me. Plus, I still got the pocketknife Daddy Blu gave me before I left."

"You really need to leave before things get worse."

"Ma, I'm your daughter. I will kill him, trust me."

"Do you need me to be on my way?"

"No, Mama. I'm okay, trust me."

Davonna and I talked until it was time for her to go to work, then we hung up. I told Marcus what was going on, and he was ready to go to Atlanta. Marcus loved my kids to death, and he would kill anyone who hurt them. I knew Patrick hadn't changed; that's why I begged Davonna not to go. It was only a matter of time before something like this happened.

Patrick is a sick, perverted fuck! He needed to be in jail or in somebody's casket. After a month of Davonna being in Atlanta, she had saved up enough money to get her a car. The car she really wanted, her credit wasn't good enough. That's when she told me that Patrick had co-signed for her a car. I was pissed because I knew the type of person he was.

"Davonna, you shouldn't let Patrick sign for you a car. Soon as he gets mad or you piss him off, he's going to take it from you. Them people are scandalous, I'm trying to tell you."

SHERRI MARIE

"Mama, you don't have anything to worry about. I'm going to make sure I pay my car payment and insurance on time, so he won't take my car."

"I still don't think it's a good idea. I know how they are."

"I know, Mama, but I already did it now."

I shook my head. "Okay."

Patrick was the type of person who does good things for people to cover his ass or to feel like he got control of them. Soon as they pissed him off, he would take everything back or throw it in their face.

Time had gone on, and Davonna was living her best life. She was stacking her money and working her ass off to get her own apartment. I was proud of her; I just didn't trust her staying with Bonnie and Patrick. Every day, I would tell Davonna that she needed to hurry up and get her own apartment. Something seemed to happen every day, and Davonna would call to tell me. She told me how Patrick kept telling her she was cute, and she was built like a stallion.

I asked Davonna where Bonnie was when Patrick was saying that, and she said, standing right there. I bet you any amount of money that Bonnie didn't see anything wrong with what Patrick said. If Patrick was making passes like that to my daughter, I knew for a fact that he was doing it to my niece Dymond.

"Ma," Day-Day said as soon as I answered my phone.

256

I could hear in her voice that something was wrong.

"Oh lord, what happened now?"

"Listen to this! Me and Grandma had gone to the store. When we came back, we had to knock on the door because Grandma left her key. We were knocking for a long time before somebody opened it. We walked in, and Patrick had Dymond massaging his feet."

"What!"

"Right! You know I said something. I was like, 'why are you massaging them big gorilla feet?' and Patrick began to laugh. I didn't find anything funny, Mama. I was so mad when I saw that. I told Dymond to get up."

"What Bonnie say?"

"Nothing. She was standing there, just looking."

"Typical, Bonnie. I bet you my last dime she didn't see anything wrong with that. Something is really wrong with her."

"I know, right. Oh, and Mama, why my door looks like it's been tampered with."

When Davonna said that, I knew it was Patrick. I knew he hadn't changed; he was repeating the same thing he did to me.

"What you mean?"

"It's hard to explain. I'm going to send you this video I took when I first moved in, then I'm going to send you a video of the door now."

"Okay."

Davonna hung up and sent me the videos. In the

first video, I could see that the door was completely fine. It opened and closed with no problem. In the second video, the door wasn't closing all the way, and the lock wasn't working. The only reason Davonna had a video when she first moved in is that she sent it to show me how nice her room was.

After I watched the videos, I called Davonna back.

"I see exactly what you're talking about," I told Davonna. "Put a towel or a piece of paper in the crack of the door. If it is on the floor when you wake up, he is coming into your room at night."

"Oh my God, that's so creepy, Mama. I'm starting to feel uncomfortable here. What if he's molesting Dymond?"

"I don't put it past him. Nine times out of ten, he is, but we don't have any proof."

"I swear, if I find out he is touching my little cousin, it's going to be a problem."

"Let's just pray he's not."

The next day, Davonna called and told me the paper she put in the door was on the floor. I already knew it would be before she even called me. The next day, she put a towel in the door, and when she woke up the next morning, it was on the floor. I told Davonna to make sure she slept with her pocketknife under her pillow every night.

Davonna said that one day she was sitting in Dymond's room, talking to her with the lights off.

Patrick walked in but didn't know Davonna was in there with Dymond. Davonna said when Patrick saw that she was in there, he tried to play it off like he was coming to check on Dymond, not to mention it was two in the morning. After that happened, Davonna started sleeping in Dymond's room sometimes just to make sure nothing happened to her.

The nights Davonna slept in her own room, I told her to put a chair behind her door. Davonna told me the only chair she had in her room was a lounge chair, so I told her to push the lounge chair behind her door. That same night, Davonna put the chair behind her door and set a flip flop on top of it. When she woke up the next morning, the chair was pushed away from the door, and the flip flop had fallen on the floor.

Davonna was creeped all the way out after that. She kept telling me she wanted to move, but she didn't want to leave Dymond and Lil Daniel. Davonna began to realize that Patrick was a creepy pervert, just like I told her. At night when she was sleeping, she would feel like Patrick was standing over her and watching her. Davonna became so scared she thought about getting cameras in her room.

One day Davonna, Bonnie, Dymond, and my nephew, Lil Dan, had come to Cincinnati to visit for the holiday weekend, Memorial Day, to be exact. I was excited, and I couldn't wait to see them. I hadn't seen my niece and nephew in years. Soon as my mother got there, she got on my damn nerves, and I was ready for her to go the same day. It seemed like she was nitpicking about everything.

KEE, MY NIECE, DYMOND, AND I WERE SITTING IN MY BACK yard having a good time. That's when I asked my niece if Patrick had done anything to her. At first, she was hesitant to tell me, but I promised her I wouldn't say anything. Dymond informed Kee and I that Patrick came into her room at night and touched her. Dymond also admitted that Patrick has said perverted things to her.

Before she could even tell me the rest, my mother told Lil Daniel to tell Dymond to come into the house. My mother knew she was outside telling me something. I wanted to go into my house and beat my mother's ass, but I knew that would be a bad idea. When I told Davonna what Dymond told me, she was devastated. I told Davonna to make sure she kept a close eye on Dymond, so we could figure things out. I wanted to approach Bonnie with the situation, but I knew that would've been a waste of time. Plus, I promised my niece that I wouldn't say anything.

"Mama, that's exactly why I don't want to leave Atlanta. If I leave them, who is going to protect them? Nobody. I feel like God put me there with them for a reason, and I'm not leaving," Davonna said as she paced the floor.

"Okay, Davonna, I understand. We need to come up with some type of plan so Patrick can get caught."

Kee, Davonna, and I brainstormed on some ideas before it was time for them to go back to Atlanta. We decided to buy some cameras for Davonna and Dymond's room. Davonna told me that as soon as she got paid, she was going to purchase the cameras.

When they left to go back to Atlanta, I could barely sleep after what my niece told me. I was so worried about Davonna, Dymond, and Daniel; it was driving me crazy. I just prayed that everything went well.

Days after they got back to Atlanta, my niece, Dymond, opened up to Day-Day. She told her that Patrick comes into her room at night. Some nights he would lay in the bed with her and ask her to have sex with him or if he could touch her. Dymond also admitted that Patrick often touches her breasts, vagina, and her butt. Dymond said she would tell Patrick to stop, but he still did it.

Davonna called me crying. She was ready to kill Patrick after what Dymond told her. I told her to stay calm because we were about to catch him in his act real soon. I knew we had to play it smart because Patrick was nowhere near dumb. Two days before Davonna was about to purchase the camera, things took a turn for the worse.

Patrick had questioned Dymond about Day-Day. He asked her if Day-Day had said anything about him, and Dymond told him yes. Patrick asked what she said, and Dymond told him that Davonna said she didn't feel comfortable around him. I don't know what made Patrick question Dymond, but he did. That caused a huge argument between Patrick, Day-Day, and my mom.

Davonna played it smart and recorded the whole argument. The entire argument, my mother was on Patrick's side.

"Davonna, why you don't feel comfortable around Patrick?" Bonnie asked with a stank ass attitude.

"Because he kissed me when I was asleep, and he be coming into my room at night, that's why."

"You a damn lie. Nobody kissed you!" Patrick shouted.

"Why you didn't tell me he kissed you?" Bonnie asked.

"Because, Grandma, you wouldn't believe me, that's why."

"How you know if you never bothered to tell me what he did?"

"Did you believe Ravine?"

"Ravine was lying," Bonnie replied.

"So, my mama was lying too, Grandma?"

"Yeah, she was lying. Your mama said she was saying that because she was mad at Patrick," Bonnie stated.

"Did you believe my mama when she told you what Patrick was doing to her?"

"Your mama said she only said that because she was mad."

It was sad that Bonnie still was taking up for Patrick after all these years.

"Your mama a damn lie. I never touched her. So, you my daughter?" Patrick asked.

"Oh, I know I'm not your daughter because my mother knows who my daddy is, and she had a DNA test with him."

"Exactly. She said you was my baby. Then the baby she killed after she had you, your sister, they thought it was mine. The DNA came back, and the baby wasn't mine."

Patrick was making up all types of lies, anything to make himself look good. After Patrick raped me, the next day, I was removed from my mother's home. I didn't see him until years later when Kee, Tracy, and I went to Atlanta. So how in the world was I pregnant by him and had an abortion after Davonna? And if Day Day was supposed to be his daughter, why didn't they do a DNA test with Day Day but did one on the baby I supposedly killed? Make it make sense, the lies they tell. Bonnie was on the recording, agreeing and lying right along with her husband.

"What about when Patrick hit my mama in the car and put her out on the highway?" Davonna asked.

"Sherri hit him first while he was driving. Your mama jumped out the car on her own and ran," Bonnie replied.

Really, Bonnie? You mean to tell me I jumped out the van on one of the busiest highways and didn't get hurt or killed? Girl, please. That don't even sound right. Tell your lie to someone who will believe it.

"What Patrick do to her to make her hit him? She didn't hit him for no reason," Davonna questioned.

"I knew you came down here with a motive. You came down here to start some shit!" Patrick shouted.

"You gave me a motive when you kissed me," Davonna replied. *"Tell grandma how you been touching on Dymond."*

Davonna wasn't backing up from Patrick, no matter how aggressive he tried to get. Patrick had a bad temper, and he often got aggressive to try to scare people.

"I never touched Dymond a day in my life!" Patrick shouted at the top of his lungs.

"If he touched Dymond, why didn't she tell me?" Bonnie asked.

"Because she's scared, Grandma, that's why."

"Dymond is not scared of me."

"It's not you she's scared of. It's Patrick."

"Dymond is not scared of him. If he was doing something to her, she would tell me."

"Well, she didn't tell because she was scared. I mean, look at his big self."

I guess Bonnie was giving Davonna a nasty look because I heard Davonna say, *"Why are you looking at me like that, Grandma?"*

"Because you a liar."

"Why would I lie to you? You my grandma. I would never lie to you."

"You just did," Bonnie responded.

When I heard that recording, I wanted to drive to Georgia and beat some sense into Bonnie's ass. I had never been so mad in my life. What type of woman would let this happen to her child and grandchildren? The thought was sickening to me. A man better not even look at my children the wrong way, or I would act a fool.

Bonnie, Patrick, and Davonna went back and forth on the recording for a while. Bonnie told Davonna to get out of their house since she didn't trust her man. Davonna packed her belongings and put them in the car.

Patrick ran outside and tried to take the car from her just like I told her he would do if she pissed him off. He even took the cap off the tire to let the air out. Davonna was mad because she didn't want to leave Dymond and Daniel there with them, but she had no choice.

AFTER EVERYTHING HAPPENED, DAVONNA AND I GOT IN touch with Chuck, Dymond and Daniel's father. We told him what was going on, and he was ready to kill Patrick. One thing about Chuck, he didn't take no shit when it came to his kids. Chuck was a hood nigga, but he had turned his life around for the better. He told me that he wasn't going to say anything to Patrick yet because the kids were coming over for the weekend.

Chuck knew that if he said something to them, he wouldn't get to see his kids. It was bad enough that Chuck barely got to see them because my mother kept them away from him the majority of the time. All I worried about was getting my niece and nephew safely out of that house.

The weekend came, and Chuck got both Dymond and Daniel safely in his arms. Bonnie and Patrick thought they were doing something by letting them go to their daddy's house because they were trying to cover their ass, but we were ten steps ahead of them. We already knew they weren't going back once Chuck got them.

Days after that, my mother and I had words because she swore up and down that I was the one who called children services and the police on them.

Bonnie: I know y'all the ones who called children services on me.

I was talking to Marcus when Bonnie texted that to my phone. I told Marcus I was about to text her and cuss her out because I was tired of her. Marcus told not to text her, but instead to call on three way so he could hear what she said. I dialed Bonnie's number and waited for her to answer the phone.

"Hello."

"What you talking about?"

"What you talking about?" Bonnie said with a nasty ass attitude.

"You keep talking about I called the police and children services on you. No, I didn't, but I should have."

"If you didn't do it, you know who did. It probably was your daughter."

"That's how I know you don't know me well because if I called, I would tell you."

"Y'all keep lying on my husband because y'all want him."

"Who lying on him?"

"All y'all."

"Your husband didn't molest Ravine?"

"Nope, she was lying."

"So, I was lying too, Ma?"

"Yap, you were mad because Patrick wouldn't give you what you wanted."

"So, was his cousin, Keila, lying too?"

My mother didn't know I knew about Keila because I never brought it to her attention. Keila was his first cousin, who he molested years ago, causing his mother and aunt to fall out.

"She said she made that up because she didn't like Patrick." My mother stuttered over her words. "Y'all just want my husband. That's why y'all keep making up lies on him.

"Don't nobody want your ugly, gorilla looking ass

husband but you. You and Patrick are fucking sick in the head. I hope Patrick has a heart attack and dies."

"You will have a heart attack and die before he will just because you said it."

"God tried to show you that you should've been paying attention to me instead of your husband. That's why God took your kids away from you, so you could open your eyes and see what your husband was doing. He gave you custody of your grandkids, and you still let the same thing that happened to me happen to them. Don't you see it?"

"Why God didn't take you? You were the one getting molested and raped, not them."

When Bonnie said that, I lost it.

"You and your fucking husband are sick! Both of y'all can suck a dick with y'all stupid ass."

"You're not going to disrespect me on this phone," Bonnie stated.

"Girl, you disrespected me when you let your husband come in my room to molest and rape me. So, fuck you."

My mother hung up the phone. I was so mad that I couldn't stop pacing the floor. I wanted to choke Bonnie and watch her die slow.

"Wow! Baby, I'm so sorry I told you to call her," Marcus stated.

For a minute, I forgot he was on three way with me.

"I told you she was an evil little troll."

"I can't believe she said that to you. We should've been recording her ass. Damn, boo, I'm sorry."

"You don't have to apologize, boo. It's okay. I needed to get that off my chest anyway."

After I hung up with Marcus, I texted Bonnie.

Me: I apologize for disrespecting you, but I don't have anything to say to you until you leave Patrick.

Bonnie never texted back, but I didn't care. I haven't talked to her since. I knew I shouldn't apologize for her behavior, but I didn't want to block my blessing. Plus, the bible says children obey your parents in the LORD, for this is right (Ephesians 6:1). That was a bible verse that was repeatedly instilled in me when I was younger.

Dear Rapist,

Why did you molest me? Why did you rape me? Why did you come to my room every night when you had my beautiful mother in your bed? Why did you suck on my breasts? Why did you stick your finger in my immature vagina? Why, when I told you to stop, you didn't? Why, when I said no, you didn't listen? Why me? Why anyone?

Those are the questions I always wanted to ask you. I want you to know that what you did to me destroyed me as a little girl. You took away my childhood. You took away things I should've experienced on my own. Most kids remember fun times and good memories of their childhood life. All I remember is pain and sorrow. I can't really recall one good moment that I had with you or my mother. You were supposed to be the second father figure to me. Instead, you were my molester and rapist.

For years, I hated you. For years, I wanted you to die. For years, I prayed that bad things would happen to you. I wanted you to be tortured, just like you tortured me. I wanted you to feel the pain and hurt that I felt. For years I had flashes about what you did to me, and it made me sick to my stomach. Your ugly gorilla face repeatedly played in the back of mind. Every time I had a flashback, I was ready to come and kill you myself. So many times, you were dead, and you didn't even know it. I used to picture you inside a casket and imagine you meeting your father, Satan, at the gates of hell.

What you did to me might've bent me, but I can assure you it didn't break me. I thought I would never forgive you, but through the grace of God, I did. If I didn't forgive you, you would still have complete control over my life. Forgiving you was one of the hardest things I ever had to do, but it was the best thing I ever did. After praying and getting closer to God, I learned that I had a purpose.

I just want to say you might have taken my child-hood, but you can't take my purpose. God has given me the ability to help other children who are going through what I've already been through. Jesus gave me the strength to tell my life story that will touch millions of people's lives. Jesus gave me the ability to start my outreach program that will help millions of children who are facing sexual abuse. Jesus gave me the ability to start my Testimony Publications company so survivors could tell their stories. Jesus turned my abuse into a purpose. I want to let you know you don't have to answer to me, but you must answer to God on judgment day. You will reap what you sow.

Galatians 6:8 Whoever sows to please their flesh, from the flesh will reap destruction. Whoever sows to please the spirit, from the spirit will reap eternal life.

Revelations 21:8 But the cowardly, the unbelieving, the vile, the murderers, the sexually immoral, those who practice magic arts, the idolaters, and all liars—they will be consigned to the fiery lake of burning sulfur. This is the second death."

Dear Mother,

For years, I hated you, but not as much as I hated your husband. I hated you for not believing me, I hated you for not protecting me, I hated you for letting me get touched every night like a grown woman. I hated you for not taking me away from the situation. Why didn't you believe me when I told you that Patrick was molesting me? Why didn't you leave him when I told you he raped me? Why didn't you protect me from the situation? Those are questions that used to repeatedly play in my mind. I blame you as well for everything that happened to me.

From eight to fourteen years old, all I wanted from you was to be protected. Instead, you called me liars and made me look like the bad person to everyone else. You painted me to be this fast little girl who was sexually active when that wasn't the case. You made people hate me and look at me differently. You even tried to turn my own sister against me with your lies, but thank God, my sister saw the truth. Even though you did all these things to me, I still love you with all my heart.

At the end of the day, you are still my mother. Like the old saying goes, sometimes you have to feed people with a long handle spoon and love them from a distance. That's exactly what I do when it comes to you. I hate that our relationship must be distant, but it is what it is. After getting closer to God, I learned to forgive you, but I will never forget. I thought that one day we could rebuild our relationship until I learned that you were the same person from years ago.

When I learned that Patrick was molesting both of my nieces, you didn't do anything to protect them. Instead, you called them liars and painted them to be the bad person just like you did me. As a grandmother, you should've protected them. Their mother, which is your daughter, is dead. I would think that you would do everything in your power to keep your grandkids safe, but I was wrong. Instead, you turned your back on them when they needed you most. What is it going to take for you to realize that your husband is a child molester and a rapist? No matter how much you try to cover it up, God knows the truth.

I know you can't be in this much denial that you don't see what this monster is doing to all these inno-cent little kids. A blind man can see through him, so I know you can. I'm starting to believe that you know what's going on, but you don't want to accept it. What is it, Bonnie? Are you scared to be lonely? You're afraid of what people will say about you? The only thing that you should be afraid of is judgment day because your day is coming.

Me, Ravine, Dymond, Patrick's first cousin, and even his three-year-old grandson at the time said that Patrick was molesting us. All you did was sweep it under the carpet. That's not sickening to know that your husband is not attracted to you, he's attracted to kids? You really don't see anything wrong with this picture? If not, you are as sick as he is, and both of you need to pay for it.

When you first met Patrick in Mississippi, rumors were floating around that Patrick was a child molester and a rapist. His own baby mother, Lisa, wouldn't even let his own daughter be around him because she knew what he had done. She protected her daughter, Nia, like a mother should've. Like you should have done.

When Nia got older and decided she wanted to have a relationship with her father, she came to stay with y'all, only to find out that Patrick was molesting her three-year-old son. Your exact words to me were, "I don't believe Patrick did nothing like that to him." Bonnie, you even said that Patrick said he was already accused of being a molester, now he was a homosexual molester, and you found that funny. You didn't see anything wrong with that picture, Bonnie?

I just want to let you know that you will eventually reap what you sow. All the children that your husband hurt, their blood is on your hands also. You can hide what you know from everybody else but remember this one thing. God knows the truth, and so do I. He knows your heart better than you do. God sits up high, but he looks down low. I pray that you ask God for forgiveness because your days are numbered. I'm praying for your soul, Bonnie. I forgive you but will never forget.

Mark 9:42 But whoever causes one of these little ones who believe in Me to stumble, it would be better for him if a millstone were hung around his neck, and he were thrown into the sea.

Psalms 11:5 The LORD tests the righteous, But the wicked and the one who love violence His soul hates. Upon the wicked He will rain coals; Fire and brimstone and a burning wind *Shall be* the portion of their cup.

UPDATE ON MY LIFE

With everything that I've been through, I'm still able to tell my testimony. I thought I would never get to finish this book because it was so painful to write, but Jesus helped me through it. Although I had some tough times in my life, that didn't stop me from pushing. I am now a published author of thirty books. Twenty-nine of those books are urban fiction. I have an associate degree in business administrative management. I have finally gotten my outreach program off the ground this year, which I have been working on since 2009.

My outreach program is called We Believe Outreach Program. This program will give information to youth who are dealing with or have dealt with sexual abuse. It will also encourage them to speak up. The outreach program will provide mentoring services, support, confidentiality, and other professional services.

I'm set to speak with children in elementary schools this year about good touch and bad touch. I also have a publishing company called Testimony Publications and plan to start taking submissions in the spring of 2020. Testimony Publications is for people who want to tell about something they overcame in life. Whether it's sexual abuse, drug abuse, domestic violence, overcoming the street life, etc. Whatever your testimony is, I want to help you publish it. I also wrote a children's book called Good Touch/Bad Touch that will release in 2020.

Marcus and I are planning our wedding and are pushing for 2021. The actual wedding date was 8/18/18 but the venue we were getting married at unexpectedly closed down months before our wedding. We felt it was a sign from God to wait a while before we got married.

FAMILY UPDATE

My oldest daughter, Davonna, who is now twenty-one years old, graduated from Mt. Healthy high school in 2016. She also graduated from Scarlet Oaks career center with a certificate in Health Technology. Davonna now resides in Atlanta, GA, where she plans to pursue her dreams as an inspirational speaker. She also has a promotion company and calls herself Promotion Princess on Instagram. Davonna gave birth to her first son, Legendary Markus Reese on April 6, 2019. I call him my stinka man lol.

My son, Quanterrious, who is now nineteen years old, graduated from Mt Healthy high school in 2018. He played football his whole high school career. Quanterrious also graduated from Scarlet Oaks career center, where he got a certificate in automotive technology. Tennessee State wanted my son for football, but he decided to go to Central University. Quan said that Tennessee was too far away from his family lol.

After a year and a half in college, Quanterrious had to take a leave because his girlfriend got pregnant. Quanterrious' girlfriend gave birth to their baby boy, Quayvion Monzell Love Moore, on April 23rd, 2019. He also started his own clothing line called BTG (Built to Grind) and is a supervisor at a janitorial company. Quanterrious resides in Cincinnati with his girlfriend and son.

Makayla is now seventeen years old and attends Mt Healthy high school. She is due to graduate next year. She also gave birth to her first son, Orenell James Teasley, on November 14th, 2019

Promise is now seven years old, and she attends Mt. Healthy elementary. She is an honor roll student. Promise also praise dances for Lincoln Heights Baptist Church. She very smart, pretty, and creative. On Promise's free days, she loves to draw, listen to gospel, rap, play on her tablet, and play make up.

My fiancé, Marcus, left the street life and decided to go to college. He graduated in 2015 with a degree in business administrative management. He also attended barber school for six months. Marcus will release his first book in 2020 under Testimony Publications called Surviving the Street Life, so be on the lookout. Marcus also has a candle business called Get Lit candle company that will launch in 2020.

I PRAYED

I prayed for a good man. God sent me you.
I prayed for a husband. God sent me you.
I prayed for a father figure for my kids. God sent me you.
I prayed for love. God sent me you.
I prayed for comfort. God sent me you.
I prayed for peace. God sent me you.
I prayed for my heart to heal. God sent me you.
I asked for a praying man. God sent me you.

I just want to say thank you, Marcus baby, for every-thing you have done for me. Thank you for sticking by me when times were good and when they were bad. We've had our ups and downs, but we made it through the storm. Long as we have faith in God and each other, we are unstoppable.

A WORD FROM THE AUTHOR

Being sexually abused was one of the hardest things I ever had to face in my life, and it also was the hardest thing to overcome. Sexual abuse turned me into a person I didn't want to be. I became angry, hateful, and vengeful. I didn't care who I hurt because nobody cared when I was getting hurt. I was always fighting and not caring about the consequences. I had to step back and look at my life in order to change my ways. I say that to say this: whenever you are facing trials and tribulations, don't give up. If God brought you to it, he would bring you through it.

Don't let your past keep you from being who you want to be. If you are going through something or have gone through something tragic in your life, don't let it hold you back or make you be the person you know you're not. Turn your story into your purpose or testimony. There is somebody out there who needs you just like somebody needs me. Don't give up, no matter what your situation is. God put you through things for a reason. Put God first, keep pushing, and the rest will fall into place. I know it can be hard at times, but the sun will eventually shine after the storm. Put God first, keep the faith, and watch how things work out for you.

The End

Please continue to the next page>>>>>>>>>>>>

WE BELIEVE OUTREACH PROGRAM INFO:

Email: webelieveoutreachprogram@gmail.com
Facebook page: We Believe Outreach Program
Instagram: We Believe Outreach Program

TESTIMONY PUBLICATIONS INFO:

Email: testimonypublications@gmail.com
Facebook: Testimony Publications

Author/books info:
Email: authorsherrineal@gmail.com
Facebook page: Author Sherri Marie
Facebook fan page: Author Sherri Marie AKA
Rere Neal
Facebook reading group: Author Sherri Marie (The
Drama Queen)

Books by Sherri Marie

Made in the USA
Columbia, SC
07 June 2022

61406671R00167